Out of the
Dog House

Turning a $1,100 Investment into a Billion-Dollar Profit

Dick Portillo
with Don Yaeger

TRIUMPH
B O O K S

Library of Congress Cataloging-in-Publication Data

Names: Portillo, Dick, author. | Yaeger, Don, author.
Title: Out of the dog house : turning a $1,100 investment into a
   billion-dollar profit / Dick Portillo with Don Yaeger.
Description: Chicago, Illinois : Triumph Books, LLC, [2018]
Identifiers: LCCN 2018040133 | ISBN 9781629376752
Subjects: LCSH: Portillo's Restaurant Group, Inc. | Portillo, Dick. | Fast
   food restaurants—Chicago-History. | Chain restaurants—Chicago—
History. | Restaurateurs-Chicago—Biography.
Classification: LCC TX945.5.P67 P67 2018 | DDC 647.95773/11—dc23
LC record available at https://lccn.loc.gov/2018040133

This book is available in quantity at special discounts for your group or organization. For further information, contact:
Triumph Books LLC
814 North Franklin Street
Chicago, Illinois 60610
(312) 337-0747
www.triumphbooks.com

Printed in U.S.A.
Design by Patricia Frey
ISBN: 978-1-62937-675-2
Photos courtesy of the author unless otherwise indicated

To my wife, who put up with all my crazy ideas.

And a special thanks to Patty Sullivan.
Without her help, this book would never have been finished.

Contents

1

Humble Beginnings

Long lines don't impress me; long lines that move fast impress me.

This particular long line wasn't moving fast, but I wanted to see what the fuss was about. TCBY, an American chain of frozen yogurt stores, had opened in 1981 in Arkansas. The company began franchising the following year and stores were being built around the country at a rapid pace, and one opened near our home in Oak Brook, Illinois.

My wife, Sharon, thought we needed to invest in TCBY. I had never been in one of their stores, but Sharon, myself, and my parents—who were in visiting from Florida—had been out for dinner and we usually stopped somewhere for dessert. We decided to get in line with other customers and try a frozen yogurt.

When we reached the counter to place our order, I knew immediately it was not a brand that we'd invest in. I told Sharon, "See those machines?" She said, "Yes." I explained it was a simple concept, too simple in fact, and pretty much everyone is going to have a machine like that. There's no science behind it. It was an easy approach that competitors can quickly copy.

I was right.

New frozen yogurt establishments were being built and TCBY's sales cooled off after its strong start. In 2001, there were 1,777 TCBY locations across the country. By 2011, according to newspaper accounts, there were just 405, and TCBY was listed among America's disappearing restaurant chains by *USA Today*.

That's why I built what I called a "moat" around Portillo's. That moat protects Portillo's from the competition, the enemy. The moat is the complexity of the business. It is filled with ideas and our core principles and it makes it very, very difficult for the competition, the enemy, to cross the moat to get to Portillo's and duplicate our business model.

History has shown that when somebody gets a good idea everyone's going to jump on it and think they can do it better and all that. So, I had to make mine so unique and complicated but at the same time it had to be trainable. In other words, it couldn't be so complicated that the average person that's in this business couldn't grasp what I was trying to do with the culture.

That moat has allowed Portillo's to maintain a competitive advantage over its competitors and protect our long-term profits.

We have come a long way from the 6' x 12' trailer hot dog stand I opened in Villa Park in 1963 from which we sold hot dogs, fries, tamales, and soda. "The Dog House" had no running water and was launched with $1,100 in savings that Sharon had earmarked for "a house with a white picket fence" but grew to average more than $8 million in sales per restaurant annually, with our largest-volume locations doing more than $17 million in annual sales.

We are famous for our Chicago-style hot dogs, Italian beef sandwiches and the creative décor of our dining rooms. No two Portillo's restaurants have the same look. To some people, it would make sense to use the same set of plans, at least from a financial standpoint. But that is not what I wanted or envisioned for Portillo's. If you walked into a McDonald's or a Wendy's across the country, it would probably look the same as any of their restaurants in the state of Illinois.

What I had to do was create something that was more unique, more interesting than what they were doing at McDonald's, Burger King, Wendy's, and others. I had to separate myself and get out of that way of thinking. People told me, "Well, you know, McDonald's does this and McDonald's does that." But I responded, "I am not a McDonald's. I don't want to be a McDonald's because I don't want to think like they do." It was a different ballgame. I had to establish something that's so different than McDonald's and Burger King and all those other guys who don't even know how to compete with me. The average Portillo's has higher sales than the average McDonald's— and that's without us serving breakfast.

Remember, the restaurant business is not just about the food. The restaurant business should be an experience. I wanted every one of our restaurants to offer a unique customer experience. When you walk into a Portillo's, you're going to see something, you're going to see colors, you're going to see an energy, you're going to see movement. The focus has to be on the customers, the people in your community who you serve. That will be a theme throughout my book. One of my favorite sayings is, "The customer is the foundation of our business."

In the 50 years I owned the company, we experienced significant growth, adding locations across Illinois, Indiana, California, and Arizona. We employed over 4,000 people and, in addition to our employees, we create work for carpenters, plumbers, bakers, drivers and equipment companies. A much broader sector of the community has benefited from the growth of Portillo's.

Customers returned the love. In the years since we first opened, there have been three major economic downturns in America. But through each of them, Portillo's sales grew! Other businesses were closing, but our customers so enjoyed the experience we gave them that our restaurant sales increased through those dark periods.

While people have lost millions trying to compete with me, I made millions—and much more.

I sold Portillo's to Berkshire Partners, a private equity firm in Boston, in 2014. The amount of money I was paid for 38 Portillo's and Barnelli's units made it the largest sale in restaurant history in the United States for its size.

Twenty-four private equity groups wanted to purchase Portillo's. There were days I had two meetings a day to listen to presentations. One would start at eight in the morning, the other at four in the afternoon. This sounds strange. I knew we were good. I knew we were successful. But once the word got out that we were for sale, it just went crazy.

But Portillo's is complex. It took years for me to get where I'm at. I purposely, by design, created something very, very complex. Specifically, my time in the Marines gave me mental toughness, discipline, taught me the value of training, teamwork, and organization, and gave me confidence. All these qualities have proven essential in my journey through life. Some people may not believe this, but we spent very little money on marketing at Portillo's. I invested that money into people.

I am humbled to be able to celebrate our achievements and my story. It truly has been an incredible journey. One might say I have lived the American dream, but it did not start that way.

The son of immigrants from Mexico and Greece, I came from a poor family and at one time thought I didn't have anything to offer the world. We lived in public housing until my father made enough money to move us to a better neighborhood on the west side of Chicago. Ultimately, he was able to purchase a home in Bridgeview, 13 miles southwest of Chicago.

As a child I was spanked and got the belt from my father when I did something wrong. I learned at an early age—when my dad said, "The world doesn't owe you a damn thing, you'll have to earn it"—that I was accountable for my actions and that I had to accept responsibility for poor decisions that I made. This is a lesson that carried over to business as well. Still, everything came hard for me in high school and I was unsure of myself. To this day I still think I had an attention-deficit disorder. My friends would study for a half hour and retain everything. I studied for two hours and learned half of what they did.

I played football and even crowned and kissed the homecoming queen in the gymnasium in front of the whole class. Many years later a classmate of mine said I probably would have been voted "Most Likely Not to Succeed."

I thought I was destined to a career of odd jobs and unskilled labor.

I enlisted in the Marine Corps seven days after my high school graduation from Argo Community High School, Class of 1957. My two years at Camp Pendleton, California, in the 1st Marine Division, represented some of the most important years of my life.

The lessons I learned under a young officer named Barney Brause, whom I remain friends with today, helped mold me into the person I am today.

We were just a bunch of lonely kids in the Marine Corps. When Thanksgiving arrived, it was the first time I had been away from home on a holiday. I was the only Marine in our Company not asked to Thanksgiving dinner by an officer, or NCO. I was thinking, "Man, I must really be a screw-up."

As I laid on my bunk in my skivvies, the door flew open and Brause walked in. He said, "Portillo, get dressed. You are coming to my house for Thanksgiving dinner." Brause had only been married five months and lived in an apartment off base. It was his first Thanksgiving dinner with his wife, Jorgine, but he treated me like a rock star, like I was somebody special.

That one moment of kindness had a profound impact on me and I have never forgotten it. I learned a lot from Brause about what makes an effective leader. He had the respect of his men and retired a full bird Colonel and served two tours of duty in Vietnam.

When I returned from my tour of duty with the Marines, I married my high school sweetheart, Sharon. And I worked the same day I got married (until noon!). I saw no reason to take the whole day off. I held 14 jobs in the first 18 months I was married. I worked day and night.

I unloaded box cars, worked for the railroad, the post office, a junkyard. I probably worked in almost every factory in the Clearing Industrial District on Chicago's southwest side. All of those jobs were back-breaking, and I knew I couldn't do that for the rest of my life. Sharon also was working during the day as a waitress.

Our dream, Sharon thought, was to purchase a house. But I knew I couldn't go back to school. I realized I had made a mistake in not preparing myself for the future. Young people think they are physically indestructible, and I realized at age 23 there wasn't any truth to it. Sharon was pregnant with our second child and I thought, "This is it. I better act now."

There seemed to be a hot dog stand on every corner in the city of Chicago, but that wasn't the case in the suburbs. I did not know anything about hot dogs or owning a business but that was the cast line I threw into the water in my search to build our future. Sharon wasn't happy about it and even talked to her mother about the decision. Her mother said, "Sharon, just be happy that you have a husband who wants to make something of himself and not let life pass him by." Sharon couldn't believe her mother took my side.

We were in this together.

In April of 1963, with our savings of $1,100 and an equal $1,100 investment from my brother, Frank, I had the first trailer built in Villa Park. It was built by Sharon's father, her father's neighbor, and me. I was scared to death. I had never even made a hot dog before or steamed a bun. We ate more than we sold the first couple of days and Sharon, in fact, said we needed to close the place until we learned how to make a hot dog because it was embarrassing. I called it "The Dog House" and it had its own theme. It was meant to look like a storybook house.

And what a story this journey has turned out to be.

Portillo's has come a long way from my wife and me preparing all the food, serving all the customers, and doing all the cleanup at the age of 23. We had no running water so I connected garden hoses 250 feet across the parking lot to another store to get water for the steam tables. When Sharon was at the stand to work, I took my infant sons, Michael and Joe, to other fast-food businesses to find out where other restaurants purchased their supplies. We bought our buns, condiments, and hot dogs from the supermarket. Back when it was just

Sharon and me, you'd better believe we had every motivation to turn the business into a success—it was all we had.

The difficulties and hardships did not deter me because I had a passion for what I was doing. I believe that if you don't like what you are doing, you shouldn't do it. You should find something that you like—something you are passionate about—and do that. If you don't have enthusiasm in what you do, it's not going to work. In everyday life, when you get up in the morning, we have choices to make. Most people get up in the morning and only think about that day. Not the future. They don't set goals.

You have to set goals in life. When you reach that goal, don't be satisfied. Set another goal. When you reach a goal, it gives you a tremendous amount of confidence. With that confidence, you can accomplish so much more in life. Even with the passion I had, I knew I needed to hire the best people in the community to make Portillo's a success. My philosophy has always been to hire the best people you can get, train them to the best of their ability, give them a complete job description and then follow up.

William James, a psychologist and philosopher, said the deepest principle in human nature is the need to be appreciated. And I believe that. We all want to be appreciated. It doesn't matter if you work for a hot dog stand, a restaurant company, or a hospital. If you show your employees that you appreciate their hard work and dedication, you win their respect and loyalty. Many of my employees worked for me 20, 30 and some more than 45 years. Our turnover rate was a fraction of the average turnover in the restaurant industry. I'd like to think it was because I am a warm and fuzzy guy (I know that's not true) but I respect my employees and I think they respect me.

Our business grew in the 1960s and 1970s. I graduated from the trailer to restaurant buildings. By 1967, The Dog House was a success and ready for a new look. We renamed it Portillo's and moved into a new building in Villa Park. When everyone my age was out partying and going to ballgames, I was working. I had no life, only work. In the early 1970s, I had my first office in the basement of our second restaurant in Glendale Heights. I had one desk, one filing cabinet and one office employee in Glenda Knippen, who stayed on over the years and was eventually in charge of employee benefits.

Even back then during those humble beginnings I realized the Portillo's culture was shaped by four core principles—quality, service, attitude, and cleanliness. This culture was part of the moat that protected Portillo's from the competition, the enemy (I will explain more about the moat later). At Portillo's we are always trying to meet the demands and the needs of the customers. During one of the many speeches that I give around the country, I have told audiences that Sam Walton, founder of Wal-Mart, taught his CEO that the company doesn't exist for the glorification of its leaders. It exists for its customers.

Another one of my favorite sayings is, "We don't need a leader who reads a balance sheet better than he reads people. We need a type of leader who rolls up his sleeves, brings everybody together, gets them united behind the strategy to solve the problems, makes sure that they're invested, and then works alongside them to ensure that it gets done."

This is true for any business in the service industry, including Portillo's. As I mentioned—and will continue to mention—I stress quality, service, attitude, and cleanliness to my employees. I would rather cut off my pinkie finger than skimp on quality because I know that's important to customers. And it's important to me.

When a family decides to go out for dinner and makes the choice to come to Portillo's—let's face it, there's a lot of competition and choices out there for families—it should be a positive experience from the minute they arrive until they leave. I often told my supervisors that I don't want to beat the competition, I want to intimidate them. And how do we do that? By doing it better than the competition does it, from the moment our customer walks through our doors. The food quality, service, and experience should be outstanding—every time—with no exceptions. Customers have come to expect higher standards from Portillo's. We have become a symbol of excellence thanks to the efforts of our dedicated employees.

Our customers are the lifeblood of this company. If they decide to stay away, we're out of business. If we give our customers exceptional service each and every time, it will take us from good to great. Superior customer service is essential. If our employees greet customers with a smile, thank them and get them what they want quickly and courteously, we can earn customers for life. And if customers for some reason don't enjoy their experience, it's also important to encourage them to come back for a better experience.

Ideas are easy, execution is not. And the needs of our customers drive us to innovate, innovations that started years ago and continue to this day.

We had to be different than anyone else. What had to be different than the TCBY yogurt shop that I walked into for the first time years ago after dinner one evening with Sharon and my parents. Portillo's is complex. It's a complex business.

To meet the customer demand for faster service, Portillo's first drive-thru opened in Downers Grove, our seventh restaurant, in 1983.

That went back to serving the customer in a timely and organized manner to alleviate some of the stress in their lives. Years ago, there was an article in *Forbes* magazine that said, "When a customer places an order at Portillo's there's a methodical chain reaction that occurs." That would best explain our system, and it's entirely customer-driven.

Customers also wanted more menu options and we responded. We introduced the Barnelli's Pasta Bowl concept (variety of pastas with homemade sauces, gourmet salads and sandwiches) in 1993. We introduced nationwide shipping to all 50 states in 2000 and added my daughter-in-law's chocolate cake to the menu. She made the chocolate cake for our family gatherings and it was so good we added it to the menu and sold over 6 million in 2017.

Over the last two decades, while I owned the business, we expanded in California (2005), Indiana (2006), and Arizona (2013) due to so many requests from loyal customers who grew up in the Chicagoland area and relocated to other states. Prior to the sale to Berkshire Partners, the Portillo Restaurant Group was the largest privately held restaurant group in the Midwest. There were no partners, no investors, and no franchises. Nobody believed how profitable we were—the business was debt free starting December 16, 2010.

After I built the first trailer in 1963, I was constantly looking for new ideas, new ways to get the customers excited about Portillo's. My mind never slept. Every time I created something different, something different that I knew the customers liked, I saw the smile on their faces. And when I saw that my ideas were working, as crazy as they were, thinking out-of-the-box, I gained more confidence in myself, and it gave me more passion. My passion and confidence grew.

And the moat that surrounded Portillo's grew and was strengthened by our success, protected us from the competition, the enemy. My moat is the complexity of the business and it helps keep the competition away. Our large menu and various processes, which include preparing beef, peppers, and sauces at massive commissaries, differs from other chains.

People say we're in the hot dog business. We're a restaurant, we're in the food business.

We have hot dogs. We sell a lot of them: 60,000 to 70,000 pounds a week. But we sell over 200,000 pounds of Italian beef a week. We have two kinds of chicken, two kinds of fish, two kinds of sausage, salads. A person can go in a Portillo's and eat something different every day. So, I wanted to get into something that the masses could do often.

There's something for everybody you know but at the same time it is quality food.

It's also a unique experience.

When you walk into a Portillo's restaurant I wanted to touch all your senses. You see colors, you see sights, you hear the music. The noise in the background, employees calling out the orders, "Number one, you're the one. Number two, this is for you." So, all that sound, that energy, the lights, and the smell of the food. It was an expensive ordeal, too. To open a Portillo's is not cheap. You have to have a hell of a lot of money to compete with Portillo's. You are going to spend $5, $6 million on just the training, the research, the construction, the land. It's not an easy concept, but that's by design.

That's the moat that has long protected us.

I remember one time Jim Cantalupo was in line at my restaurant in Downers Grove, which we opened in 1983 as our seventh restaurant and was relocated in 1997. Jim—standing in line next to construction workers and soccer moms—served as chairman and chief executive officer of McDonald's Corporation until his sudden death by heart attack at the age of 60 in 2004. Jim told me, "You know, if you could ever simplify this, you could open a lot of these places but it's very complex."

I told Jim that I didn't want to simplify it because that will invite competition.

No single person can make an organization successful. It's the employees who help win us customers for life. Who would have thought back then that we would end up creating thousands of jobs and opportunities over the years? With the hard work and dedication of our employees, it turned out to be so much more.

Retirement doesn't interest me. I love the challenges and excitement of business. I have never been on the golf course, have never picked up a club. And I am not completely out of the food business as I serve as a paid consultant to the Portillo's chain for Berkshire Partners.

I am also an investor in other restaurant chains. Additionally, I have purchased retail, apartment, and industrial properties, and I am still shopping for more. I don't like to spend a lot of time behind a desk. I also would like to spend more time with my grandchildren and children. That could not happen if I would have remained in the position I was in.

The community has embraced and supported Portillo's and I will never forget that. I can't imagine doing anything else. I have a passion for what I do, a love for my family and a deep appreciation for the support of my community. I feel blessed to have been able to pursue my dream, and it's an American dream that continues every single day of my life.

I can't wait to share that journey with you in this book.

2

Family Struggles

We had it all, in terms of family heritage.

My mother, Stravoula Docas, came from Greece by way of Ellis Island and my father, Frank Portillo Sr., was from Mexico. While Mom was 100 percent Greek, Dad was part Spanish, Mexican-Indian and French.

Our family today smiles and jokes we probably could fly every flag some day of the year—and in every Portillo's restaurant. My wife is Polish, Lithuanian, and Russian. My son, Michael, married a Sicilian-and-Irish gal. And our granddaughter married a German Englishman. That's basically the United Nations!

My parents had what at the time seemed a traditional love story. They met in a tannery on Goose Island, an artificial island in Chicago that is formed by the north branch of the Chicago River and the North Branch Canal. This island wasn't known for its sand, sun, and palm trees. Far from it.

That batch of land had long been an industrial area. Tanneries, soap factories and lumberyards flourished there at one time. Yet it has been said that it could be a dreary place even on a sunny day.

Mom and Dad were married August 31, 1929, a few months before the Great Depression. Great timing, right? It was the longest, deepest, and most widespread depression of the 20th century. Chicago was a tough place in those days. Many people in the city were unemployed and became dependent on food handouts. If you look at Chicago's history, many turned to crime as a way to deal with poverty.

Both of my parents were uneducated—neither graduated from grammar school. But they were good people and raised on hard work. That's all they had known their entire lives.

Dad was born in Durango, Mexico. He moved to El Paso, Texas, with his sister, Carmen, and their mother, my grandmother, Trinny. Dad's older brother Julian already was in Chicago at that time. Trinny cleaned houses and cooked for a mining company. Dad and Carmen helped clean houses, too. Once Julian saved enough money in Chicago, he purchased a train ticket for Dad. Dad was 15 years old when he moved to Chicago and lived with Julian, who was seven years older.

Why did Dad move to Chicago? Honestly, I have no idea. I know Chicago over the generations has been the destination point for many immigrants, especially Eastern Europeans and Mexicans. There were jobs in Chicago, from farming to the steel industry to the meatpacking industry. I have a great photograph of Chicago in the 1920s. I blew it up and it has the Wrigley Building and the Tribune Tower, an aerial view and right behind it now it's all lofts and condos. But back in the 1920s it was all industry, smokestacks. It was an industrial life that offered opportunity to guys like my father.

Mom was born in Greece and came to Chicago in 1920 with her grandmother Virginia. I am telling you, Grandmother Virginia was the toughest woman I ever saw in my life. I hardly ever saw her smile. Most people's grandmothers are sweet; my dad's mother was sweet and kind.

Dad was a salesman, but he also worked in any kind of factory in Chicago that made stuff. Later he also sold insurance and even was an instructor who administered driving tests. It's not a secret that I came from very humble beginnings. I was born at 1330 West Van Buren Street in Chicago and was the youngest of three children behind Frank and my sister, Carmen.

During my childhood we moved to a public housing row house on Mohawk Street called the Mother Frances Cabrini Housing Project. That's a polite way to say we lived in the projects. It was bad and dangerous. The walls were so thin that you could hear the conversation in the next room, even hear the person going to the bathroom. You could hear the echo of gunshots outside. People looked down on you when they found out you lived in the projects.

Of course, money always seemed to be an issue in our family. I remember there was a retail store, Montgomery Ward, right around the corner from the projects. And my mother stole a pair of shoes from the store for either my brother or me, I can't recall for whom. But the whole neighborhood found about it and my mother and father got into a loud argument, yelling at each other. Really, the only time they ever argued was over money. I recall my mother saying, "Well, if you made enough money I wouldn't have to do that." If you knew my mother, she's like Mother Teresa for crying out loud. I never heard her swear. She was a kind, wonderful mother, what everyone wants a mother to be. I am certain she stole those shoes out of love. Any mother probably would do the same thing if their child needed shoes.

There was another time when my parents were low on funds and they had to sell my tricycle. I think I was around five years old, and I still remember that tricycle. It had black handlebars and red steamers on it. But we had to live and eat, right? I also remember one Christmas when I really wanted an electric train. Marshall Fields, on State Street, had a huge display window out front with this electric train on the tracks going around a Christmas tree. I was like, "Oh, God, an electric train. Holy crap." I knew I would never get an electric train for Christmas, it was out of the question. I thought maybe a plastic wind-up train might work. You wound it up and let it go; and wind it back up when it unwound. So, I hinted to my parents about a train for Christmas.

Dad was a skilled carver. He really loved to carve, and to this day I have a lot of his wooden carvings in my home. That Christmas when I hinted around for an electric or wind-up train, I ended up with a carving of a train engine and a caboose under the tree. I was disappointed and Dad knew I was disappointed. But shame on me! This is the God's honest truth. If I had them today, that carved train engine/caboose would be one of the most valuable items in my collection. And I've got Picassos and other valuable art. Dad couldn't afford to buy me an electric train or a plastic wind-up train that Christmas; instead he gave me a gift he made from his heart with his hands.

As a kid, you have to adjust to your elements. It also was hotter than blazes in the summer with all those stone buildings and cement sidewalks in the projects. The heat was hellish. So, we'd pack up and go to the planetarium in Chicago. There was a slope that went down toward the water, and we'd spread out blankets on that slope and feel the breeze off of Lake Michigan. We'd sleep there because it was so much cooler.

I don't recall ever going on vacation, but I know we made the 800-mile trek from Chicago to Vineland, New Jersey, one time because my mother had an aunt who lived there. We stayed in their house and went to Atlantic City one day. That was our family vacation.

Every time he could, Dad moved us to a better neighborhood. From the government subsidized housing on Mohawk Street, we next went to 1617 South Central Park, another part of the west side of Chicago. It was a better neighborhood but not the best place either. Our building was infested with roaches. Our bathroom walls were white and I remember one time I got up and flipped the light switch on. It was like a kaleidoscope with the roaches moving along the walls. When that neighborhood started to change for the worse, Dad made enough money to purchase a house in Bridgeview, a southwest suburb where my life started to come into focus.

One thing that was not lacking in the Portillo household was discipline. I got the belt from my father when I did something wrong, and that's when I learned every decision had a consequence. I always say that my dad had an opinion on corporal punishment: he was in favor of it! I thought my dad was hard on me, but that was nothing compared to boot camp when I enlisted in the Marines after my high school graduation. Between my dad's discipline and the drill instructor at boot camp, for the longest time I was convinced no one liked me. But I realized after a while that my dad was trying to teach me right from wrong, and the drill instructor was trying to make a good Marine out of me.

Frank is six years older than me. He was always a hard worker. He built a house when he first got married—I helped him dig the foundation for it. He also went into the restaurant business, but we took different paths that had different results.

Frank married his high school sweetheart and worked as a drafts-man at Northern Illinois Gas Company. He was promoted to a field engineer but knew any potential advancement was limited without a college degree. He went to work at Brown's Fried Chicken on the weekends and asked the owner, John Brown, a friend of our father's, to sell him the right to build a second restaurant for $1,000. When Frank couldn't get a business loan, Brown agreed to partner with him.

Frank opened his first store in 1958. Frank and Brown were doing well and, by 1963, franchised five more restaurants with employees. By this time, I had returned from my tour of duty in the Marines, gotten married and worked countless dead-end jobs before deciding to open a hot dog stand.

Sharon and I put in $1,100 and Frank matched our $1,100. He was a partner on paper only for about four months. At that time Frank said, "Dick, this isn't working. Why don't you buy me out?" And I did. The franchise boom had started by then and Frank went his way, and I went my way. Frank grew the Brown's chain to 100 stores by 1987. But the competition was intense. Kentucky Fried Chicken, which had opened in 1952, was one of the first American fast-food chains to expand internationally. In 1991, Frank began serving pasta with each meal and renamed the restaurants Brown's Chicken & Pasta.

Two years later, the restaurant unfortunately was in the news after two suspects entered the store in Palatine around closing time and murdered the two franchisees and their five employees. Print and tele-vision media described it as a massacre, frightened customers stopped coming and the crime went unsolved for nearly 10 years. It was a bad time. It was admirable of Frank to try to help find the murderers but it took a toll on him and the business. Business dropped at least

40 percent, according to media reports, forcing dozens of locations to close. Two men were eventually sentenced for the crime and, in 2009, Brown's Chicken & Pasta Inc. filed for bankruptcy protection following a legal dispute between Frank, the majority owner, and the company's minority owner at the time. Frank's retired and living on St. Pete Beach in Florida.

My sister, who was nine years older than me, died of breast cancer more than 30 years ago. Carmen was an angel on earth. Everyone loved her. She was very religious, very spiritual, beautiful physically, mentally, and emotionally. Carmen married a pathologist but she never thought to get a mammogram. During her chemotherapy treatments I asked her, "Why didn't you get a mammogram?" She said, "Well, I didn't drink, I didn't smoke, I led a good life." Carmen found the lump in her breast herself and died 14 months later. It happened that quickly.

I got along great with my sister. She was just the kindest, most generous woman I have ever met. I mean, everyone loved her. When she died, her wake and funeral were enormous. People came from all over because they just loved her.

Carmen had two things on her bucket list that she wanted to do: one was to go to Greece and the other was to see the renowned Greek composer and performer Yanni. Fortunately, I was in a position to take care of both those things for her. We went to Greece and went on a cruise to the Greek Islands. We landed in Athens and got to see some of our relatives who still live in Greece. We got to see Yanni when he performed in Chicago. We had great seats, second or third row, and had a wonderful time. Carmen was a wonderful person.

My mother lived to be 90 years old and my dad lived to be 98—he would have lived longer if he had taken care of himself! Dad enjoyed fishing and loved reading. That is where he got his education from—books. He really loved history, and I don't think he ever read a work of fiction. Maybe that's where I got my love of reading from. I am just like Dad. I love to read and I have never read a fiction book, because I know it's not true.

I remember we held Dad's 96th birthday party in our backyard, and he sat in a chair under an umbrella smoking a cigarette, nursing a shot of Jack Daniels, and reading his birthday cards. The guy never wore glasses or took a vitamin. He was a good-looking guy with a full head of hair.

I actually made him give up cigarettes because I was afraid he was going to fall asleep with one in his hand and burn the house down. He'd take a nap a day and nothing bothered him. But I finally had to take the car from him when we found out he was driving down the wrong side of the street one night. I told him I had to have the oil changed in it. When he asked later where the car was, I reminded him we were having a lot of trouble with it.

Dad never had a lot of pressure on him. He told me the only time he really had a lot of stress in his life was when I was in high school. And Mom was kind and gentle and understanding to the kids. I didn't spend a lot of time with my parents growing up because I was always off doing my own thing. But they were wonderful parents.

Of course, my best memories were in high school at Argo Community High School, 7329 West 63rd Street, in Summit. I recently donated $1 million dollars to the school and years earlier was recognized as a Distinguished Alumnus. When school officials notified me of the award, I thought it was a joke. I was the guy in high school who wore T-shirts with the sleeves rolled up and jeans. I was quite the rebel. I told the *Chicago Tribune* that "I don't know who nominated me, but it was quite an honor." I was amazed at the school computers, weight rooms, the four gymnasiums and new athletic fields.

You know how some people look back on their college years as their best years? I never went to college. I look back at high school. I have a lot of great memories, a lot of fun memories. But I also wasn't the best student. I got in my share of trouble for fighting and misbehaving and spent time in the principal's office explaining myself. I also had time for football and was on the line—I played center, tight end, and defensive end.

Sharon and I were high school sweethearts. She was supposed to go to a high school closer to her home, but her family didn't like it so she attended Argo. Not to brag, but I also dated a lot of girls before I fell for Sharon. One of those girls was Phyllis Breider. She was one of the most popular girls at the school. Smart. Cute. A cheerleader. But her parents just hated me. Hated me. And I hated them.

I remember one time I borrowed my father's car and I planned to take Phyllis to the movies or something like that. It was raining pretty hard when I pulled up to her family's house. We didn't have cell phones back then, so I couldn't call Phyllis or send her a text to let her know I had arrived. I knocked on the door. Mr. Breider opened the door and looked at me. I said, "Hello Mr. Breider, I am Dick Portillo here to pick up your…"

I never got to finish.

Boom! He slammed the door in my face.

So now I am standing out there in the rain. I had on a pair of jeans, nice shirt, white socks, loafers, leather jacket. I thought I looked pretty good. The door opened, and I am soaking wet now. It was Phyllis. She told me not to pay any attention to her father. We still went out that night. But we nearly had to sneak out every time we wanted to go out. I dated Sharon, Phyllis, and a couple of other girls before I enlisted in the Marines after my high school graduation.

That's when I got the Dear John letter from Phyllis. I would give anything, a ton of money, to still have that letter today. Phyllis said that her parents finally convinced her that I wasn't the right guy for her, that it was a waste of time for her to date me and that I would never amount to anything. It went on to say, "Dick, after looking at you, you never took classes seriously," and that she had met a lot of young men in college that really wanted to do something with their lives.

And blah, blah, blah. She ended the letter by saying she was breaking up with me.

Of course, I don't have any regrets and wouldn't change a thing. I worked my behind off, building a multimillion-dollar business from one hot dog stand. I had plenty of motivation from my childhood and upbringing in the projects to do the very best I could. A lot of people looked down on me, but I made it.

And I made a better decision by marrying Sharon.

3
Life in the Marines

I graduated from high school on June 3, 1957, at age 17. Since I didn't plan to attend college, I had one option—and it really wasn't an option. If you didn't attend college, you were required to enlist into the service. That was Uncle Sam's law.

I am not sure why we don't still have that obligation in the United States. We're the only industrialized country in the world that doesn't have it. I think that's a mistake. Personally, I believe the opportunity to serve your country is an honor and great for a young person. Every kid should spend some time in a branch of service.

It was good for me. I learned valuable lessons that shaped me personally and professionally. When you arrive in boot camp, everyone's going in different directions. But by the end of it, everyone's moving at once, in unison. It's all about the training. You are able to follow orders and think under stress. It taught me that if you spend enough quality time with the average person, they can be trained and a plan will work.

That's not to say I was in a hurry to enlist. I didn't want to go into the Army. I didn't want to go into the Navy. I didn't want to go into the Air Force. The commitment to those service branches was three to four years. The Marine Corps, however, was short of men at that time and it wanted to shore up its enlistments and offered a two-year commitment.

My buddy John Zajda is the one who told me about it. He said, "Dick, we're going to go in one way or another—and sooner than later—so let's do it now."

On June 10, 1957—seven days after I graduated from high school—I enlisted into the Marine Corps.

So long Chicago, hello California.

The trip was a big deal for me. I had never been on an airplane. I really never had been outside of Chicago other than when my dad drove us to Atlantic City. Vacations weren't part of summers in our neighborhood. Florida might be called the "Sunshine State"—I have a home in Naples in southwest Florida—but I didn't know anyone who had vacationed there while I was a child.

I was in awe when I boarded the TWA flight for San Diego. The plane had four engines. I thought, "Man, I just went from Chicago to California in eight or nine hours with one stop." I was so impressed.

When we arrived in San Diego, a civilian told us we would eat lunch at the El Cortez Hotel. It was the tallest hotel in the city when it opened in 1927, sitting atop a hill at the north end of downtown. I remember the waitress asked me what I wanted to drink and I said, "I will have a beer." She said, "Okay, what kind?" This woman had to know we were all young, underage kids, but everyone ordered a beer.

I had one beer, then another, followed by a third. We were having a good ol' time. Of course, it was about that time when somebody mentioned there was a green Marine Corps bus outside the hotel with some mean, nasty looking guys on it. We were told we needed to get on that bus. Now! We laughed, joked, and smiled as we headed to the bus. I had three beers of fun in my belly—and no idea what was about to happen next.

We filed onto the bus and one of those "mean, nasty looking guys" told us to wipe those smiles off our faces. They said if we had gum in our mouths, swallow it. Sit down and listen, they said. Their message was loud and clear. The good times were over. There were 75 of us in our platoon in San Diego. The moment we stepped foot into that facility, we were basically cut off from the civilian world and trained to adapt to a Marine Corps lifestyle.

What was that lifestyle? It was stress, yelling (and more yelling) and running to get into shape. It was living in barracks and tents with no air conditioning. It was about being told where to be and what to do. The training focused on a variety of subjects, from weapons training to Marine Corps history. Everything we did was for a purpose, an oft-repeated and rehearsed purpose. The psychological transformation of boot camp was intense and intentional.

But it also taught me about teamwork and organization. The lesson that impacted me the greatest was learning to think and make decisions under stress. I can't stress enough how fundamental but important that was. But, man, I couldn't wait to get out of the Marines. I counted down the days from the moment I walked into training camp. I didn't like anyone telling me what to do.

Even the training "games" weren't for the timid and had a purpose. I remember one time when our platoon and another platoon were lined up on opposite sides of a 50-yard field. A large ball was placed between us and the goal was to get the ball. Rules? What rules? This game didn't have any rules. The object was to get the ball over the line, by any means necessary. The drill instructor blew his whistle to start the game. Imagine 150 guys stampeding at each other, separated only by that large ball. Guys were fighting, kicking, and swinging at each other—that was part of our training. I remember I was on the ground and I looked up, and there was the ball, all by itself.

I was a combat engineer in the Explosive Ordinance Disposal (EOD) Company in Camp Pendleton. Have you ever watched the movie *The Hurt Locker*? It was a 2008 movie about an Iraq War EOD team that was being targeted by insurgents. The technicians who disassembled those explosives had a support team around them. I was part of the support team, the muscle that helped protect the technicians, and a lot of guard duty.

I didn't have much confidence in myself when I joined the Marines. I often thought I was a screw-up. And while in the Marines, I found new and creative ways to screw up during my two years. Have I told you about the time I and Zajda got locked up in a Tijuana, Mexico, jail?

John and I had a 1948 four-door, stick-shift Chevy. We knew when "boots"—guys fresh out of boot camp with short-cropped hair and a scared look on their faces—were waiting by the bus stops in San Diego, they were headed to Tijuana, a border city in Mexico, just south of California, about 30 minutes away. All the guys wanted to go to Tijuana because it was known for its nightlife. John and I had a deal that we'd drive four guys to Tijuana for $20 each. We'd drop them off at a bar called Maria's Place. A few hours later, we picked them up and returned to San Diego. We did that a couple times of week, so that was a lot of money in our pockets.

One particular trip, after we dropped off the guys, I was driving down a side street in Tijuana. I ran a stop sign and hit a Buick with those big fenders on it. When it happened, I had a flashback to our classes at Camp Pendleton, where we were instructed not to go to Tijuana. But, if you did go, make sure you didn't get in trouble. Instructors shared case histories of Marines and sailors who ended up in jail—not only in Tijuana, but in big Mexican jails—and families had to mortgage their homes to get their kids out.

So, I instantly remembered those lectures as the driver in the Buick was screaming at me in Spanish. But I also noticed the fender on the Buick where I hit it was bent against the wheel. That was going to make it difficult for him to drive his car. I looked over at John and said, "Let's get in the car and we'll get the hell out of here."

And we did—or so we thought.

There was only one way out of Tijuana, but it was a weekend and the cars were lined up to leave the city. We left the guys at the bar because, hell yeah, I was scared. I didn't want to get in trouble. They were Marines and would figure out how to get home, which they did. But I knew it was crazy for me to stick around after the accident. We were edging toward the border when I noticed this guy coming up with a policeman. I rolled down my window but kept driving slowly in the bumper-to-bumper line.

The policeman said to me, "Please, señor. This man says you got in an accident?" I answered, "Oh, no. I didn't get in an accident with him." I was still driving slowly, edging along because I wanted the hell out of there. The policeman asked me to put the brake on, then finally said, "I think you should get out of the car," as he put his hand on his gun. I pulled over and the policeman wanted to assess a $700 fine. I asked the policeman if he planned to hold court right then and there.

"Si, señor," he replied.

Seven-hundred dollars, especially in the late 1950s, was an awful lot of money. We didn't have that kind of money on us. I was told the car would be impounded next to the Tijuana police station. I wanted to make sure we'd get it back, so I asked the policeman to confirm we would if I paid the $700.

"Si, señor," he replied.

I can't recall how we got back to the base, but we did. John and I went back to Tijuana the following day with a Marine who was Mexican and spoke Spanish fluently. He had a car. I didn't have $700 but I had some money on me. We found the Tijuana police station where the car was impounded. The lot had a construction horse in front of the entrance. An older gentleman who was the watchman stepped out of a guard house. It was time to play "let's make a deal." I asked him if he would turn his head and let me get my car for $25.

He said, "No, no, no."

I asked if $50 was enough—I think that's all I had on me. So, I stressed that $50 was as high as I was going. Then I did something stupid. Very stupid. I told John to go start the car. I picked up a brick as I was trying to convince him to take the $50. (Another one of those moments I can't be proud of.) He started to scream and ran back inside the building. At this point, the Marine who came with us took off on foot. John had trouble starting the car, but it finally turned over and started. I was trying to move that wooden horse in front of the entrance.

All of sudden I heard, "Alto!"

I turned and there was a handful of Mexican cops pointing their guns at us. That is the God's honest truth. I thought, "Holy crap, what is my dad going to think?" They handcuffed both John and me. It just so happened the old man I threatened with the brick was the father-in-law of one of the policemen. This wasn't pretty. They dragged me up a few steps into the jail. One policeman had one of my legs, another policeman the other. My face bounced off the steps and I was hit by batons and kicked. We spent a day and a half in a Tijuana jail. There's nothing worse than a Tijuana jail.

Thankfully, the Navy got us out. Yes, the Navy helped a Marine.

The Marine who was in Tijuana with us made it back to base and talked to a Sgt. Cisneros. Cisneros knew there were officials in the Navy who worked with helping Marines and sailors, and they got us out. I ended up paying the $700 to get our car back. But the story doesn't end there. The Marines had a say, too. My punishment for the Tijuana escapade was a two-headed coin. I was given mess hall duty and had my liberty card pulled (a liberty card is your ticket off the base).

Mess hall personnel wear different uniforms than the green and khaki colors of a Marine service uniform. You wear whites and a paper hat and work from morning until night. We fed thousands of Marines three meals a day. The worst part was, I thought my mess hall duty was only 30 days. As I waited for the relief truck one night, I was told by the driver that my name wasn't on the list to be returned to my EOD company at the end of my 30 days. The driver said, "Oh, you got another 30 days." I was really pissed off, but I deserved it.

Still, I obviously didn't learn my lesson.

One day while guys were going through the chow line and I was dishing out food, two guys from another barracks—they were from Chicago—talked about going out that night to drink some beers. I told them I had my liberty card pulled and was confined to the base. They said, "We will sneak you out in the trunk." I was working 15-hour days and I figured what the heck, let's do it. I got dressed in civilian clothes and hid in the back of the trunk. We had a case of small beers in 8-ounce and 10-ounce cans and went driving around Oceanside, north of San Diego.

It was fun until the Oceanside police pulled behind the car—we were speeding—and pulled us over. The guys were able to dump their booze before we were stopped. Of course, I didn't have my liberty card, which prompted a call to the Military Police. And I also had a beer that I didn't throw away. Talk about stupid. I ended up in the Oceanside jail for one night and the next day until late afternoon. But it was a helluva lot better than Tijuana.

I am telling you it had reached the point to where I got out of bed just to see how I could screw things up that day.

I had two extra days added to my mess hall duty, making it a 62-day total. Plus, I was put in a place called the scullery, an area used for washing trays. It was the worst job in the camp, just terrible. We had to scrape off the leftover food on the metal trays, rinse them and stack the trays so they could run through this huge dishwasher. I was in charge of the scullery and one of my duties was to make sure the temperature on the dishwasher remained at a certain level. But it was so hot in this place that I lowered the temp on the machine. Mistake. The water wasn't hot enough to remove all the grease from the trays.

We had all these racks of trays and a mess duty officer and a sergeant walked into the room for an inspection. The officer with him, a second lieutenant, ran his finger across a tray and his finger had grease on it. He threw the tray down. He took another tray out from the same rack and it had grease on it. He went to the next tray. Grease. He knocked over the entire rack of trays. He says, "Who's in charge of the scullery, sergeant?" He answered, "Portillo, sir."

The second lieutenant proceeded to spread grease across my fore-head and up my nose. Yes, up my nose. The second lieutenant didn't get a good grade on the inspection, and he blamed the mess sergeant. And, naturally, the mess sergeant blamed me. This guy really had it in for me. Not only was I still in the scullery, but I now had to hand scrub the cans where they dumped the trash. I also had to hose it down after the scullery was cleaned. It was so hot and so smelly, just awful.

One day as I took a break out back in a shady spot, smoking a cigarette, the mess sergeant's wife drove up in a car. And the mess sergeant came out from the mess hall and placed some stuff in the truck. He was stealing. I went up to him and said, "Sarge, where is that going?" He answered, "Well, we don't have to talk about that, do we?" I said, "Hell, we don't. This is illegal, you know."

That was my ticket to an easier job in the mess hall. Ultimately, I got a really cushy job when I got off mess duty: I became a captain's driver at Camp Pendleton. I also was promoted to a Lance Corporal because the captain I drove around didn't want a PFC behind his wheel. I even had a Jeep with my name on it; God's honest truth, I have a photograph of it. Corporal Richard Portillo. I'd run information to the Marine Corps headquarters and do whatever the captain wanted. I'd wait outside smoking a cigarette while he was in a meeting. I really liked that job.

My two years in the Marines, when you look back on them, was an amazing experience that helped shape me. I learned about the way leaders treat people, and nobody was better in that area than Lieutenant Barney Brause. As I mentioned earlier, he was probably one of the finest leaders I have ever met in my life.

I faced a lonely Thanksgiving after I joined the Marines in 1957. All the other new recruits had already left the barracks with invitations from family or other officers to enjoy a Thanksgiving dinner. I was ready to head to the mess hall when Lieutenant Brause came in and invited me to his home near the base to eat dinner with him and his newlywed wife, Jorgine.

That memory has stayed with me my entire life, and it was an experience that influenced how I treated my own employees. I learned a lot from him on how to treat people. He was tough but he still treated people well. I watched him a lot after that dinner and saw how he spent time in training. If you screwed up under his watch, you were in trouble. But his Marines would jump off a roof for this man. I would.

Brause was incredibly brave. Here are a few examples of that bravery his son Scott shared with me:

"As you mentioned, Dad was with the Provincial Reconnaissance Units in his second tour of duty in Vietnam. This operation was part of the secret Phoenix program run by the CIA. We have a photograph of Dad with South Vietnamese marines in the jungle holding a "skull and crossbones" notice in Vietnamese that was placed on enemy bodies, warning the VC of their fate if they did not leave the area.

"In his second tour of duty he saved the life of Chesty Puller Jr., after the lieutenant stepped on a land mine and had both legs blow off above the knees. Dad put his fists into the man's groin to staunch the hemorrhaging and held them there until medics arrived. If this image of war doesn't make you cringe, consider this: Dad told me that in the previous days he had repeatedly let Lt. Puller know that he needed a haircut, and that the lieutenant (either while lying there or from his hospital bed, I can't remember which), said: 'Colonel, how do you like my haircut?'"

When someone is kind to you, it sticks in your mind. My family knows about this story, too. And I always thought about what happened to him. So, I had my office track him down and found out he served two tours in Vietnam and retired a full bird colonel and lived in Southern California. I wrote Barney a letter and explained to him how many years ago he was kind to a young, homesick kid from Chicago. I told him I wanted to reciprocate and take him and his wife on a first-class, all-expenses-paid trip to the Solomon Islands on a chartered yacht with a crew. And we did. We met in Fiji and went from Fiji to the Solomon Islands. We became good friends and stay in touch. I have taken him on several other trips to places such as Saipan, Guam, and Iwo Jima.

Barney knew how to treat people. It wasn't like some of the other guys I met in the Marines. Some said I got more stripes than you, so you are nothing, so do what I say. Barney spent time talking with you calmly and made sure you understood what he wanted done and why. He was able to sense if you didn't understand him. If that was case, he'd stay on a particular subject until you understood it.

He treated us like human beings. We loved this guy because of his leadership abilities. There are leaders who try to lead with fear and some because of respect. I've always believed that respect is like an invisible chain that holds people together. It's proven in history that leaders who try to lead by fear are going to screw you over, because fear alone won't do it. But if you are respected as a leader, you've got something special there.

And, combined with a Marine's discipline, that's how I wanted to lead my business.

4

Moving Back to Chicago

So long California, hello Chicago.

The moment I fulfilled my two-year obligation to the Marines, I returned to Chicago. And I returned, too, into the arms of my high school sweetheart, Sharon. I visited Sharon when I was on leave and we stayed in touch through letters; those letters were far different from the Dear John letter I got from Phyllis while I was in the Marines.

It's funny how life sometimes happens for the best. I am so lucky Sharon is in my life. She is probably the kindest person I have ever met. Sharon is so loving about family and people, and her love is deep and genuine.

My middle son Joe said, "Dad, they don't make 'em like Mom anymore." Joe said he sees all these other mothers and women out there and Mom is special. I am telling you, God threw the mold away when it came to Sharon. She's a special lady. I ended up smelling like a rose when I married Sharon. She is perfect.

When I returned to Chicago from California, Sharon was my steady girl. And, months later, I made her my wife. I was 19, Sharon 17. Her parents didn't show me any hostility at all over the marriage because I was committed to Sharon. And, quite honestly, I think my parents loved Sharon more than me. Sharon treated them like they were her own. That's the kind of woman I married.

I first saw Sharon when she was 14 years old at the Teen Inn, a club where teenagers danced, listened to music on the jukebox and drank soda. It was the typical 1950s setup that you might see on television today. The skirts, the Bobbysocks, the saddle shoes. The club was opened early evenings Wednesdays, Fridays and Saturdays and closed around 9:00 PM. My buddy Johnny actually wanted to meet Sharon, so he asked me to go talk to her and make the introduction. I can still remember Sharon wore a blue sweater the first time I saw her.

The introduction didn't go as planned for Johnny. I asked Sharon out myself.

We went to Saganashkee Slough, a lake near Chicago in Cook County, on our first date. But the date came with strings attached. I told Sharon I first had to go to a rumble—we had a fight against guys from a rival high school. I love to fight. I can't explain it other than to say the excitement masked my insecurities. That's who I was back then and it got me in a lot of trouble.

I was a freshman or sophomore in high school and I was walking with a girl named Carol through a park. We were on the outside of the park and there were some guys taking a break from playing ball. Two of the guys were brothers, big Irish kids. The group of guys circled around me and started to make comments about Carol and shoved me around. It was embarrassing as heck to me. They pushed me down and wouldn't let me up. Carol yelled at them to leave me alone. I started to swing wildly but they roughed me up pretty good. I walked Carol home but I never forgot about that fight.

A few years later I was at the Argo Bowling Alley with Mike Corbitt, who later became the chief of police in Willow Springs. Mike, who died in 2004, became a cooperating witness after being convicted of aiding in the murder of Chicagoan Diane Masters by her husband, Alan. Corbitt authored a book about his experiences entitled, *Double Deal: The Cop Who Was a Mobster.*

I was at the bowling alley with Mike and a few other guys when I saw the two Irish brothers who roughed me up in that park. The brothers walked out of the bowling alley to Mommy and Daddy's 1956 Lincoln convertible. I never liked spoiled rich kids; most of them were spoiled brats and I figured the brothers were like that. We waited on the side of the building and I said to them, "Remember me?"

They looked around and I am sure they didn't like what they saw. The guys with me were rough and tough. And we started to pound them pretty good. Mike pulled out a knife and cut the car tires, the convertible top and interior leather. Their parents found two of the guys who were with me, but the guys wouldn't name the rest of us. There was a story in the newspaper about the incident. The parents said in the article that they feared for their sons' lives and wanted the matter dropped. Nobody was arrested. That probably doesn't happen in today's world. I was lucky.

There was a bar called Al's Fox & Hound owned by another Argo High classmate, Al Valecka. The bar had a 4:00 AM license, meaning it could sell alcohol until that time. There were two or three guys who came in early in the morning and were causing trouble. Al called Mike since Mike was a policeman at the time. Al wanted Mike to take care of the problem with this group of guys. Mike showed up and started wailing on the guys—but it was the wrong group of guys!

Yes, fighting was so stupid, but it's what we did. On that first date with Sharon, I told her I'd pick her up at the Teen Inn when it closed—after the rumble. I must have made alternative plans, too. When the club closed, Sharon sat on a back stoop. She wasn't alone. There was another girl waiting, too, a girl Sharon, a freshman at Argo High School, recognized as a senior at Argo. They didn't say anything to each other until the other girl asked Sharon who she was waiting on.

Sharon said, "Dick Portillo.' She asked the senior who she was waiting on.

"Dick Portillo," the senior said.

Well, Sharon stayed and the senior left. Sharon often wondered what I would have done if they both stayed. But some questions don't need to be answered! I showed up after the rumble and drove Sharon to Saganashkee Slough, as promised. It was cold and icy, and, being a gentleman, I reminded her to watch her step so she wouldn't fall as we walked around the lake. Naturally, all of a sudden, I slipped on some ice. Both of my feet went out from under me and I landed on my rump.

And that's how we started dating.

When we were married, we had literally nothing. I think we had a couple sets of sheets somebody gave us. But our parents did everything they could and gave us a wonderful wedding. It was held in the banquet room at…well, actually, it was in a small basement with no windows at Serino's, an Italian restaurant near Midway Airport.

We didn't have enough money to pay for a band and we couldn't invite any of our friends. We limited the reception to 90 people—family only because we were on such a limited budget and we came from big families.

Sharon's dad was one of 13 and my mother was one of five. There were aunts and uncles and cousins, because back then families were very close ethnically and everyone lived in the same neighborhood. Sharon's grandparents were born in Poland on one side and Lithuania on the other, and she also came from a close-knit family. That small basement was packed but we had a lot of fun. We had a small bar set up for drinks and had Polish sausage, sauerkraut, beef, and chicken for dinner.

Of course, some of my rowdy friends crashed the reception after the dinner. And they went straight for the bar. They already had a few drinks in them, and two of my buddies—talk about a big entrance—fell down the stairs that led into the basement. They added to the bar bill, but it was a good time.

I also worked on my wedding day. It's true. Sharon and I didn't go on a honeymoon until we were married for seven years. We simply did not have the money—or the time—to get away when we were married. I always worked to make ends meet, and most weeks it felt like 24/7.

I had a shift at L.A. Young Spring & Wire Corporation on my wedding day. The company made automobile cushion springs assemblies and wire garment hangars and such. It was piece work, which meant the faster you worked, the more money you made.

I remember one time when the buzzer went off for lunch break. I didn't bring a lunch and didn't want one. I was getting married and needed the money so I stayed on my machine. These two union guys—good ol' boys from Tennessee—approached me and said, "Did you hear the buzzer?" I said, "Yeah, I heard it." They asked, "Well, ain't you going to take a break?" I said no and explained I was getting married and needed the extra money. They didn't blink. "You know, we fought like hell for this break," they said, encouraging me to take a break. "I don't give a damn what the union says," I said. "I am getting married and I need the money. Go to hell."

That wasn't the answer they wanted.

They slashed two tires on my car. When I walked outside after my shift, a bunch of those guys stood around and said, 'Oh my god, look at the poor ol' boy. Two tires, my god. And he's probably only got one spare." Not a problem. I called a buddy, we jacked up—no, not those guys, the car—and fixed the two tires.

I did what I had to do. I had no other choice. When I returned from the Marines, I had 14 jobs in 18 months. A lot of them were part-time jobs, but I always had two at one time. And they were awful jobs, too. We did anything we could to save money.

We once lived between two canals in Willow Springs, about 18 miles southwest of Chicago. It was an attic apartment above a farmhouse and the rent was $50 a month. It was hotter than blazes in the summer. It had a big fan in the window, no air conditioning, with a small kitchen and a fold-out bed in the bedroom. The owner was a nice lady but a real busybody. She'd march up the wooden stairs into the apartment all the time without knocking. She'd look in the cabinets and the oven and around the apartment to make sure everything was clean.

We were so naïve. The owner checked the oven and mentioned how much grease was inside it. Sharon politely explained the type of cleaners she used in the oven, and the owner said, "Did you ever try elbow grease?" Sharon stood there for a moment and innocently asked, "Where do you buy elbow grease?" That's great, isn't it? Where do you buy elbow grease?

That memory still brings a smile to our faces.

This memory does, too. It was so hot in that attic apartment that I slept naked. Sharon tossed a sheet over me when she heard the owner walking up the stairs. I said, "Honey, next time don't throw a sheet over me." Sharon said "Really?" I said yes. The next time the owner walked into the apartment unannounced, Sharon said she did a double-take when she saw me sleeping naked. The owner went back downstairs and never came back up into the apartment.

When our first child, Michael, was born, we moved back to the city of Chicago. We went from an attic apartment into a basement apartment that was owned by Sharon's aunt and uncle on Natoma Street in Chicago.

It had a bedroom, a kitchen and a living room that was just big enough for a sofa and a television set. The bedroom was so small we had to take the closest door off to fit Michael's crib. We barely had enough room to stretch out. We have lived in some bad dwellings, but nothing like that one. It was very small and every day was a constant scrap to get by. It was a lot bigger than our attic apartment.

I was always looking for the next best job. I simply quit a job and moved on for a better one. The only time I was ever fired from a job was while I was in high school. It was a laundry job where I placed name tags on the laundry bags when people dropped them off.

The guy running the laundry was a piece of crap. So, what I did to get back at him was switch the name tags on the laundry bags. I was fired. When I came out of the Marines and got married, I realized that

I didn't know a thing. I didn't prepare myself for anything in life. All I could do was shoot a rifle, a machine gun and throw a hand grenade. Those skills didn't do me any good in life outside of the Marines.

I had so many terrible jobs, which made it even more difficult. I worked once for Corn Products, a large refinery in Argo, on the southwestern limits of Chicago, that made products from corn. I didn't have a particular job at the factory. Whatever needed to be done that day, I did.

Most days I had to mop the floors, which were greasy from the machinery and had a layer of starch dust on them form the dry corn. One day I saw a bunch of guys in the factory who were two to three years older than me from Argo High and in middle management. I saw them coming and hid behind a boiler because I didn't want them to see me.

Another time I was working in part of the factory where we had to shovel this germ that was part of the end of the corn onto a conveyor belt. There wasn't any air conditioning on the factory floor and it was so hot. Plus, we had to wear masks to protect us from inhaling the acrid dust from the corn. The foreman sat in an air-conditioned office, and I remember him being a nasty, swearing, booze-swigging guy. He had a bag he pulled out of his drawer with a half-pint booze bottle in it. He had gauges in his office that alerted him if the machinery wasn't working properly or to his satisfaction. He'd crack open his door and scream at us to do this or do that. He treated us like garbage.

I couldn't do much about the bosses, but I made sure my co-workers respected me. I was the only white guy in that part of the factory during my shift. The black guys working there didn't like me. Sharon made me a brown bag lunch every day, usually a bologna sandwich.

There was a shelf where we placed our lunches. One day I grabbed my bag and it was empty. The guys were sitting and smiling when I walked in. I grabbed a coal shovel and told them if it happened again, I would swing this shovel at every one of them. I said I couldn't fight them all, but I would take great pleasure in smacking one of them over the head with this shovel. And it never happened again.

I later worked in a junkyard and it was a dead-end job, too. You were treated like crap. That's when I started to realize that when management didn't treat its employees with any kind of respect, you, the employee, tried to screw it in any way, shape, or form that you could.

Ironically, one of my best paydays came on a day when I didn't go to work at any of my string of jobs. It was winter and Chicago was buried by a snowstorm. It was bad enough that it kept me from work because my car, a 1949 Chevy, wouldn't start. But I saw the snowstorm as an opportunity. I borrowed a shovel from Sharon's aunt and went door-to-door and shoveled driveways and sidewalks.

That afternoon I made $120, tax free. It was more money than I made in a day at any of my jobs to that point. Even if I couldn't get to work because of the snow, I had responsibilities and couldn't afford to just sit around the apartment and watch television.

It sure felt like all work and no play during our first few years of marriage. But I remember when Sharon and I saved a few extra dollars to go on our first nice date to a new restaurant called Richard's Steak House. Sharon was so excited. I had a 1949 Chevy that had the wings on it that opened and let the air in. We also had a unique feature in our car that wasn't part of the original design—a hole in the floorboard that allowed us to see the street.

I didn't have enough money to valet park, so we found an open space and walked into the restaurant. We had never been to a steak restaurant. Sharon was 18, the legal age to drink for the first time. She actually had her first glass of wine in that restaurant. We couldn't believe how nice it was. The dining areas were candlelit and the waiters were dressed in tuxedos. When they handed us the menu, we didn't know what to order. We had never seen a menu like this.

We each ordered chopped sirloin steak. It was the cheapest item on the menu. When our meals arrived, Sharon cut into her meal and said, "This is the most tender steak I have ever seen. Look at that. The knife goes through it like butter." I tried to be debonair and charming and said, "You know, that's the way these fancy places are."

Of course, we later found out chopped sirloin steak is hamburger. We never knew that. We had never heard of chopped sirloin steak. It had sirloin in it, so it had to be steak, right? We were just two naïve kids and it was probably better that we didn't know. We went to the school of hard knocks. It's not necessarily a degree you want, but you can't argue its value.

Now, we just look at each other, hug and say:

"Look what we did. Look what happened to our life."

I also worked at a forging plant during those first 18 months after I returned from the Marines. The forging plant was where metal was pressed, pounded, or squeezed under great pressure into parts known as forgings.

The process is normally performed hot by preheating the metal to a desired temperature. The burners were like a thousand degrees and we had to wear protective helmets and goggles, gloves up to our elbows and a hoodie. The metal was so hot that you took them out with clamps and placed it on a metal dye machine. The engineer set up the dye, you'd press a pedal and the machine slammed down.

Sparks flew everywhere and the sparks burned you despite the protective gear. I'd go home with small burns all over my shoulders, arms and back. Needless to say, it was oven-hot in this factory, too. Nearly unbearable. The walls rolled up like garage doors to let in some fresh air but nobody really noticed.

One day Sharon came with me to work to pick up my check. I parked near the building, and Sharon waited in the car while I went into the office. Where I parked, however, Sharon was able to see inside the factory and saw the forging, the machines, the sparks, and the conditions we worked under.

When I got back into the car, Sharon was upset and crying. She looked at me and said, "This is what you're doing to support the family?"

I said, "Yes."

Sharon thought the job was horrible and was consumed by tears. They couldn't wash away the reality of our situation though. At that time, it was our life.

Inside my heart, however, I knew I couldn't do manual labor forever. There had to be more to life than working dead-end jobs.

I had to figure something out. I had to create a future for us.

5

A Mother-in-Law's Approval

From the day we each said, "I do," Sharon had a vision for what marriage, family and life as a couple would look like. She wanted a house with a white picket fence and a nice yard in the suburbs. That was the American dream in the early 1960s and she shared it.

On the flip side, I realized I had made a mistake in not preparing myself for the future. I had more jobs than I could count on both hands and we moved from one bad apartment to another to save money, pennies at a time. For instance, we saved $5 a month to move two buildings over into a "garden apartment"—which meant it was in the basement—in Villa Park, a suburb west of Chicago. Our apartment was near the back of a busy shopping plaza on the corners of North Avenue and Addison Road in Villa Park.

At age 23 with two small children, I knew I had to act. And it was our shared love for hot dogs that gave me a crazy idea in 1963. Our neighborhood needed a hot dog stand, I believed. I wanted to be the one to meet that need.

I came home one night and asked her how important that house with the white picket fence was to her. She said very important. "Why?" she asked, warily. I answered, "I'd like to take that money we had set aside for the house and build a hot dog stand." I won't say exactly what she said because I want to keep this book family friendly. The discussion went to a place that's not fit to print!

There's nothing more symbolic in Chicago than its hot dog. It seemed as if you could find great hot dogs in every corner in the city, but hot dog stands were far and few between in the suburbs. It didn't matter at the time that I didn't know a darn thing about hot dogs, other than I liked to eat them and I thought we needed a hot dog stand in Villa Park.

I can still remember when we lived on Natoma Avenue in Chicago. Sharon was pushing our son Michael in a baby carriage and walked by a hot dog stand. She dug into her purse with crossed fingers, hoping she had the 25 cents to buy a hot dog. That's how difficult the times were for us.

When we moved to Villa Park, we had $1,100 in our savings account. Sharon at the time worked too, as a waitress. We literally saw each other in passing; when she arrived home from her shift, I left for mine. In a way, it was a vicious cycle with no end in sight.

But Sharon was emphatic and wanted to use our savings as a down payment for a house, not a hot dog stand. She was so upset with me that she went and talked with her mom, Josephine, about my plan. She said, "Mom, he wants to take our life savings and build a hot dog stand. Can you believe that?"

Josephine could have easily scuttled the whole idea. And who knows what would have happened to this story if she had. Would I have gone back to what I was doing? Would we have eventually purchased that house with a white picket fence and a yard in the Chicago suburbs, and still be living in it today? It didn't work out that way and I owe it to Josephine.

Josephine told Sharon she should back me up because I was working hard, job after job, and, unlike some other men my age, at least I "had ambition." She credited me with having a dream and encouraged her daughter to support me. Sharon decided to follow her mom's advice. She returned to our apartment, we hugged and sat down together at the kitchen table. She never complained, not once about that anyway, because she worked alongside me to make our dream turn into reality. And that reality involved owning a hot dog stand.

Even if that future in the beginning appeared to be short lived.

I still needed more cash than the $1,100 we had in savings to get started. I talked my older brother Frank into matching my $1,100 and becoming my partner. At that time, Frank, who is six years older than I am, worked with John R. Brown, a chicken farmer who opened Brown's Fried Chicken, a take-out restaurant that started in Bridgeview, a suburb of Chicago. In 1958, Brown partnered with Frank, and Frank and his wife opened their first store in Elmhurst. By 1963, other stores had opened, and Frank handled the day-to-day management of them for Brown.

Frank agreed to be my partner and match my $1,100.

I had the idea and the money, and now I had to build a business I called The Dog House. Years earlier I saw a picture in a magazine of a building that looked like a dog house. I thought it looked good, so I ripped the page from the magazine and kept it. It was a large building made of brick and mortar in California that sold hot dogs and ice cream.

I obviously didn't have the money to build my Dog House like the one in the photograph. Working construction was one of my 14 jobs in 18 months when I got out of the Marines, but I needed help. I recruited my father-in-law, who was a carpenter.

Aberdeen Welding in Chicago made me a 6' x 12' utility trailer bed with a hitch. My father-in-law, a neighbor he recruited and I went from there and built the wooden structure. It had a pitched roof, one door on the side of the building and one in the back, one sliding window in the front, a counter beneath it and a red-and-white-striped awning out front. We had Dog House across the front and sides of the building in big, red letters. We didn't have any seating because, well, a hot dog stand is called a hot dog stand because you ate the "red hot" while standing.

I also had convinced the village that I planned to move the trailer from place to place for charity events, but I unknowingly fibbed. I couldn't have moved it if I wanted to. I never thought about the weight of the building on top of that trailer. The Dog House was so heavy that we placed cement blocks under the trailer to hold it up. We had a skirt around the building that hid the blocks from view. That trailer wasn't budging a foot!

Thankfully, we didn't have to haul the trailer by truck very far, three blocks or so, to the parking lot of a discount store at that time called The Big R. Across the street from The Big R was another store called Tops Discount Store. The parking lot was at a stop light and it was a blue-collar neighborhood. It was the perfect place to sell a low-cost "meal."

The building lasted from 1963 to 1967, but by the end it was a mess. It wasn't made to last that long. I sold it for $750 to a guy named

Lenny who moved it to Lansing, Illinois. He went out of business and sold it to a guy in Cal City. That guy went out of business and donated it to the City of Cal City and some kids torched it.

But by then, it had served its purpose.

I didn't know how to make a hot dog the day I opened a hot dog stand on North Avenue in Villa Park in 1963.

I know that sounds like the opening to a bad joke. Sadly, it wasn't.

I also didn't have a lot of confidence in myself. I didn't know a thing about steaming a hot dog. I didn't know how to steam a bun. As I would quickly learn, the amount of steam means something. I never thought about holding a dry run to see how the hot dogs tasted. It was a small operation. We also offered French fries and a drink. I sold four hot dogs with fries for a dollar. Drinks were 10 cents. That was with a coupon.

We could feed a family for $1.50. How could we fail?

I made a lot of enemies at the beginning because truthfully the product was terrible. The buns were dry and burned. I had drilled holes through the bottom of two 12" x 24" pans and laid the buns on top thinking the steam would come through. Nope. The buns were hard as a rock. The hot dogs were overcooked. The French fries didn't have a consistent taste. Sharon said, "This is embarrassing. We can't do this."

She was right. I did everything backassward. I should have learned first. I realized I needed to find out how to steam a bun, make a hot dog and what products we needed. One afternoon I asked Sharon to watch the trailer because I wanted to take the kids to Gene & Jude's—not to eat, but for a reconnaissance mission.

Gene & Jude's is one of Chicago's better hot dog restaurants. Gene Mormino opened his first stand in 1946 and relocated in 1950 to River Grove, about 12 miles northwest of downtown Chicago. And it's still there. I have eaten at Gene & Jude's many times and it serves a good hot dog. But, of course, my business was failing during those early days because I didn't know what I was doing.

I remembered there was a storeroom at Gene & Jude's with a sign outside that said No Admittance, Employees Only. But deliverymen walked in and out and dropped off supplies. At that time, I purchased a lot of my supplies—specifically relish, mustard and ketchup, whatever was on sale—from the local food store. So, the condiments had a different taste each time. I purchased buns from the local bakery and the hot dogs from Vienna Sausage Company. I knew how much I started with, but I didn't even know what my food costs were.

I packed up Michael (two and a half years old) and Joe (six months old) and the stroller and headed to Gene & Jude's. I made my way to the storeroom entrance. I told Michael to watch his younger brother—smooth move, right? I walked into the storeroom and checked out the products. The first thing I saw was Lakeside relish, and it was the one ingredient I remembered. I wasn't in there long before a guy walked in and asked, "What are you doing here?" I said, "I am looking for the bathroom." He wasn't happy. "This ain't no bathroom. Get outta here."

It was ballsy, gutsy, or stupid—whatever you want to call it—but I got some valuable information when I walked into that storeroom.

That's how I learned. I visited other businesses too, making notes and asking questions. Everything I did was because I learned about it from somewhere else.

I learned how to steam a bun when I went to Gene & Jude's because I leaned over the counter and looked inside every time they opened the roll cover at the window. I mean, I nearly poked my entire face inside the window when I ordered. They probably thought I was weird, and maybe I was. But I was aggressive and I saw how they steamed the buns. They had a little screen but it wasn't placed on the hot metal. They also had a piece of cardboard on it, the steam came over it and they laid a box of buns on it. And boom! I found out how to steam a hot dog bun and I found the product to put on it.

When I got home, I telephoned Schweppes & Sons, a restaurant supplier that sold Lakeside relish. Gene & Jude's used it on its hot dogs. That meant I needed to use it on mine. I opened a hot dog stand but I didn't have the right mixture, the right product.

Nothing seemed easy and I am sure many people thought we'd fail. The post office did. It refused to give me an address because it said my business wouldn't be there too long. My brother Frank had a Brown's restaurant in the shopping center and his address was 635 West North Avenue. So, I just said The Dog House would be 635½ West North Avenue because I had to get mail. The post office was wrong because that address is still being used today at a Portillo's.

Frank was my partner for only four months. That was fine and there were no hard feelings. Frank was busy with his restaurants and he never actually helped in the trailer anyway. I was a one-man show unless Sharon was there to help, and she helped out plenty. I bought

Frank out and repaid him the $1,100 (in payments) he had invested into the business.

We were open from 11:00 AM to 10:00 PM (though I stayed open later if somebody was standing there with cash in hand). We opened every day with the exception of Christmas, Easter, and Thanksgiving. I was depressed those days because I wanted to be at work. Sharon was great, too. She'd help me during the lunch rush. We had an old Ford Falcon station wagon and Sharon backed it in behind the trailer. I'd lift the hatchback and the car turned day care for Michael and Joe was filled with their toys. It was like a big playpen for them. Daddy and Mommy worked—and Mommy kept an eye on the kids through the screen door on the trailer.

I was driven by panic and a fear of losing everything. I always wanted to learn more. There were days I sacrificed my own health, but it came with the territory. I mentioned earlier the one day I was so sick with the flu that I passed out in the trailer. A customer looked in and found me. He thought I was dead.

One time during the winter a car pulled up in front of the trailer. I leaned out the window and told the guy not to get out of the car, that I would bring his order to him. I mean, it was a cold and blistery night. The guy said he wanted two hot dogs and two root beers. I completed the order and asked him what he had, and he said a $10 bill.

So, I made the change and headed out the side door. There was a step block in front of the door, but I missed it with my foot. I fell down, scraped my knees and elbows pretty good and the hot dogs, drinks and money went flying everywhere. The two people in the car started to get out to help me, but I told them to get back in the car—it was too cold outside. I went back into the trailer, made their two hot dogs and root beers, got the change for the $10 and walked out carefully and gave them their order. That couple came back many years later with their own children and shared the story with them.

Finally, I knew what I was doing. I was making and selling hot dogs. I also started to think outside the box.

There was a guy who worked for a printing company and he showed up every Friday night at The Dog House to feed his family. I asked him if he had leftover scraps of paper from his printing orders and he said, "Yeah, why?" I asked him if he could print up basically what served as a coupon on those scraps of paper that said, "Four hot dogs and fries with the trimmings, $1 at The Dog House." I told him I'd feed his family a couple of times a week if he did this for me. He agreed.

One day the paper would be pink, the next day blue, the next day orange and so on. I also understood for the first time of the importance of location, location, location. Our trailer was in a prime spot, with two discount stores close by. That's when discount stores started to dominate the landscape in suburbs across the country and really became part of everyone's lives. The Villa Park neighborhood we were in could best be described as blue-collar. But there were a lot of people and the discount stores always attracted crowds because their products were inexpensive to purchase.

I put up a sign in the window at The Dog House that said be back in 10 minutes, and off I went. I put coupons under the windshield wiper of every car in our parking lot and in the parking lot across the street. When I came back, there must have been 50 or 60 people waiting in line with the coupons. I opened the window and the first customer in line said, "I will have four red hots." "Yes, sir," I answered. I dropped two baskets of fries and turned the temperature up on the steamers for the hot dogs and buns. At that point, I started to make more than four hot dogs at a time because of the demand. I thought, "God, this is a great marketing tool."

But I also realized I wasn't making any money on the sodas. I used premix, so I was basically exchanging dollars. The Dog House had electricity but not running water. I needed water to mix with the flavored syrup to create the soft drink—and a profit. But I couldn't get the water. I called my buddy John Zajda, who was a pipe fitter after he returned to Chicago. I asked John, if I placed a 40-gallon water tank in the attic of The Dog House, could he connect piping from the tank to the soda machine? He said it wouldn't be a problem.

It wasn't a problem, but it was a long Friday night and Saturday for me. We worked all night and I helped him with the pipes. I think the sun was coming up Saturday morning by the time I filled the tank with water. I had five 50-foot garden hoses that I strung together across the parking lot, from our trailer to an outside faucet at the National Food Store that was in the shopping plaza. I turned on the water, ran back to the trailer and filled the tank. John went home to bed because it was Saturday morning, but I had to open The Dog House. I was dog tired, but this dog had a smile on his face. I had sodas, man. I had Coca-Cola, I had root beer. I had a profit.

I was so excited that I had goose bumps. Every night I filled that 40-gallon tank up with water—and a profit—as I ran 250 feet of garden hose across the parking lot. It was a bitch, but now I thought I was a freaking genius. I was so smart. Who else would have thought of that? Well, I didn't pound my chest in celebration very long. The good times lasted two weeks or so. One day a customer walked to the window and told me his Coca-Cola didn't smell right or look right. It had a green tint to it.

I put a closed sign in the window immediately. I knew this was bad. The Coca-Cola didn't smell right and looked like a green river? I went into the attic and opened the tank and wow! The water was green. I never thought about how you cleaned the damn thing out. I am surprised nobody died.

One dilemma led to another. I was out of premix, which meant I couldn't serve any kind of sodas. I telephoned the salesman I had previously purchased the premix from and told him I was in a spot. He didn't have to help me out because I stopped ordering from him, but I got the premix. I think I was closed for half the day.

Chicago winters also tested my water supply. Since I couldn't get water from a frozen silcock (exterior spigot), I used a 10-gallon milk container that I got from Sharon's father, who was a milkman at one time. There was a laundry room in the basement of the apartment building where we lived. It had a washer, dryer, and a cement sink. I cut off some hose and filled the 10-gallon milk container with water, carried it upstairs and put in the back of our old beat-up station wagon and drove it over the trailer.

I think it took a month after we opened to make our first $25 after the lunch rush. I thought, "God, how exciting is this?" I know it might sound crazy and I might look stupid, but it was so exciting. And I had a feeling this venture would work. Despite the daily challenges, I always thought eventually I might need a bigger trailer. Business had started to increase. I wanted to get two cash registers instead of one.

I wanted to get two steam tables because I wanted to provide better service. Many days—and this isn't an exaggeration—I had 50, 60 even 100 people in line.

I also understood there wasn't enough margin in the hot dogs to do what I wanted to do. There simply wasn't enough profit when you sold four hot dogs for one dollar. As we progressed I knew I needed something with more margin, more profit, and more dollars that I could utilize in my cash flow.

There was a reason why I changed the name from The Dog House to Portillo's a few years after we opened. The reason came in a certified letter from a lawyer who explained there was a restaurant business in Youngstown, Ohio, that had registered the name Dog House. This business planned to open restaurants in Chicago, including down the street from our trailer.

This Dog House was a breakfast, lunch and dinner establishment that also specialized in hot dogs. It didn't have a shape like a dog house; it looked like a Greek restaurant with a lot of glass on the outside. The lawyer explained in the letter that this company owned the Dog House name and I had 30 days to change my business' name.

I was scared. I never had received a letter from an attorney, and I didn't have the financial resources to fight in court for the name. How could I fight it? I was wrong. I didn't know the name Dog House was registered. It never crossed my mind. After a long day at work, I was at our kitchen table with pencil and paper, thinking up all kinds of crazy names. I didn't want to get sued because I didn't have any money. I sat there lonely, scared, and tired, thinking of all these names like

The Wiener Shack, Wienies for You, Hot Dog Heaven, The Hot Dog Shack. I didn't know what to do.

We had a dog at the time, a dachshund named Pokey. I was at that kitchen table and I looked down at Pokey, her tongue hanging out and tail wagging. Right then and there I said to myself, "That's our new logo right there. That's it." It was a dachshund with one ear up, one ear down, tail wagging and the tongue hanging out. I penciled "Portillo's" on top of the logo.

I thought it was perfect, a good, warm story, because people love dogs, love animals. And it couldn't have worked out any better. Over time the name allowed us to expand our menu so dramatically even while Portillo's started as a hot dog stand. As for the Dog House out of Youngstown, Ohio? It went out of business. The building it opened down the street from us now sells used cars.

Remember when I said there was a time in my life when I thought fighting was exciting? Well, I had finally found my new excitement. This was the energy and passion that I always looked for. I was my own boss. I worked an astronomical number of hours but people liked what I did. That was such a shot in the arm. They liked my trailer, they liked my food, they liked my idea. And I liked them. I wanted to please them. I wanted to make my customers happy.

There was more to it, too.

Being hungry and not having money and being scared—that's when your creative juices really start to flow.

6

Time to Expand

Thank you, Harold Reskin, for taking a chance on me.

Those first few years in my hot dog trailer were difficult, but I always believed my business would be successful. Sales doubled each year and the customer lines were really long. But I only had one register and one steam table. Remember, long lines don't impress me; long lines that move fast impress me. I knew I was wasting my time and leaving money on the table in that 6' x 12' trailer. I needed a bigger trailer with running water. If I had two registers and two steam tables, I could serve twice as many people, twice as fast. Nothing else mattered in my life, that's how goofy I was. Along with those same thoughts of grandeur, I knew the ultimate goal was to move into my own building.

But this was an hour-by-hour, day-by-day journey.

Harold Reskin was a Chicago real estate landlord who graduated from DePaul University in 1953 with a law degree. He also served on the university's board of trustees for more than 20 years. He owned the Villa DuPage Shopping Center where I had my first trailer. Mr. Reskin was considered the founding father of Glendale Heights, a northern suburb of Chicago where he had a polo field on his 100-acre farm. Mr. Reskin traveled the world to play polo and was a successful businessman. When Mr. Reskin was in the area, he always stopped by my trailer for a hot dog. Mr. Reskin and I just hit it off. He always liked me for some reason, and he'd stick around and we'd talk about everything, including my plans to expand my business.

I was obsessed, quite honestly. The only thing on my mind was building a larger trailer. I had a neighbor named Lloyd Isaacson, whose wife later worked for me. Lloyd was always good to me, and he offered to build that second trailer in his driveway. He wasn't a professional builder, but he's a pretty handy guy. All I needed was the money. I saved every penny I could, but I still was $2,500 short.

I had a black-and-white composition book that detailed my sales down to the penny in hot dogs and soft drinks. I took my financial information to Addison State Bank, where I did my banking, with the hope of securing a loan. The loan officer's name was Jim, whose father-in-law was the bank's vice-president. Jim had that kind of spoiled rich kid look that I despised as a youth growing up. And, when he looked at me, he probably saw just a 20-something hot dog guy in checkered work pants who owned a small, wooden hot dog stand in a shopping center parking lot. I may not have looked the part of a successful, savvy businessman, but I knew if I had running water combined with my existing sales, I could make a hell of a lot more money in a bigger trailer.

I explained myself to Jim and showed him the figures I had written down in pencil, but he wasn't impressed. Sitting in a swivel chair behind his desk, he looked at me and said bluntly, "Mr. Portillo, do you really expect myself or members of my staff to go make hot dogs if you default on this?" Then, without saying another word, he rotated in that swivel chair and turned his back on me. He didn't even say good-bye as I got up from my chair and walked out of the bank.

Quite frankly, I was bitterly disappointed. At that point, I figured my only option was to continue to save the money myself. I knew it might take longer, but that's when persistence and determination are important. Too many people are so used to having everything given to them. That's not good. You have to learn to bounce back when you are down.

A little luck helped in my case, too.

Mr. Reskin stopped at the trailer for a hot dog and he asked how my expansion plans were coming. He said, "How are you doing with the loan?" I told Mr. Reskin the bank turned me down. He asked, "What are you going to do?" Though frustrated, I planned to plow forward. I told him I was going to save the money and build a larger trailer one day. Mr. Reskin finished his hot dog and asked me to stop by his office the following day.

I am not sure if I thought it would make a difference, but I wore a polo shirt and had all of my financial information written down in ink—not in pencil. I went through the same presentation with Mr. Reskin that I did at the bank. Early in the conversation, Mr. Reskin said to call him "Harold." That should have been a positive sign, but I was so focused on explaining how I could pay back a loan in two years and increase existing sales that I didn't notice the pleasantry.

Mr. Reskin studied my numbers for a few moments and I thought, "Oh boy, is he going to reject it?" He then pressed the button on his desk phone and asked his secretary Grace to come into his office. Grace walked in with a pencil and paper. Mr. Reskin said, "Write a check for Mr. Portillo for $2,500." My reaction was, "Holy cow." I couldn't believe what just happened.

I asked Mr. Reskin about the interest rate on the loan. He sat there for a moment in his chair and said, "I get to eat anything I want in any restaurant that you ever open anywhere in the world for nothing. Me and my family." I said, "That's it?" He said, "That's it." I agreed to the deal—and I paid back the loan in 12, maybe 13 months. In a *Forbes* magazine interview years later, Mr. Reskin said, "I loaned him the money based on no other collateral than my confidence in his abilities. I didn't know him well, but I'd watch them take home the pots and pans to wash them. I admired that and decided to take a chance."

Mr. Reskin and I remained friends until his death in 1996 at age 66 after a long illness. Two of my early restaurants were built on property owned by Mr. Reskin. Prior to his death, Mr. Reskin donated $2 million to DePaul's theater school and it was renamed from the Blackstone Theatre to the Merle Reskin Theatre, after his wife.

Thank you, Harold Reskin, for taking a chance on me.

The second trailer was nine feet wide and 17 feet long. Since it took up more parking spaces, Mr. Reskin increased my rent for the space from $100 to $200 a month. That was fine because, as I figured, business would be booming. We had two registers, two steamers and two lines (that moved fast) for customers!

Business was great despite the grueling hours. As I have mentioned, I worked every single day for three consecutive years, only closing the doors on Easter, Thanksgiving and Christmas Day, and I got off early on Sundays. But the hardships didn't deter me because I had a passion for what I was doing. Most people get up in the morning and only think about that day—not the future. You have to set goals in your life and chase them.

With two registers, I had to hire a cashier in 1968. There was a store in the Villa DuPage Shopping Center where I had my trailer called The Big R. I heard about a cashier named Pauline Abruscato who was fast, efficient, and great with customers. I watched her and agreed with what everyone had said about the young lady. I offered her 10 more cents an hour, but I warned her she'd be leaving an air-conditioned store for a hot dog stand. Pauline's boss warned her not to come with me and said, "That kid's not going to be around too long."

He was wrong on two counts. I owned my own business for 50-plus years and Pauline was one of my longest-tenured employees. Years later I asked Pauline what made her decide to come work for me and she said, "Because you appreciated my work." We all want to be appreciated. If you show your employees that you appreciate their hard work and dedication, you win their respect and loyalty. Even with the passion I had, I knew early on I needed to hire the best people in the community in order to be successful.

Looking for ways to improve service, I added a small enclosure that allowed people to step into the trailer during the winter. Business was doubling, doubling, doubling. I realized I was going to be done with trailers, that it was time to move into a building.

In 1971, I built my first restaurant on the site of my old trailer and moved the hot dog stand to another shopping center parking lot in Glendale Heights that Mr. Reskin owned. The building didn't have any seating, but it had a bathroom for employees. We had a small storage area for supplies, but business was really good and we quickly ran out of space. So, we had to put supplies in the bathroom, too. If somebody had to use the bathroom, they'd move all the boxes out, and put the boxes back in when finished.

I also was cooking the beef in Nesco roaster ovens. I'd start at 7:00 in the morning, slicing the beef and cooking it in multiple roaster ovens on the counter. The setup was an electrician's nightmare. I tripped the breakers because of an overloaded circuit. I ran too many devices at the same time on the same circuit—and the building wasn't even air conditioned! It became a daily game but electricity won. I unplugged the cooler while I cooked the beef.

I knew it wasn't the best setup—and dangerous if I wasn't careful. My insurance man, Chet Grilli, stopped by the trailer one day and saw my maze of roasters. He said there was a business in Cicero, a suburb west of Chicago, called Lombardi's that had large ovens to cook beef. He recommended I talked to the owner, Mike Lombardi, saying he was a nice guy. I did, and Mike and I worked out a deal where we both made a little money. I gave him my beef recipe, he cooked the beef, and I sliced it at the store.

Speaking of my beef recipe, I have an interesting story about it—and how I hired and fired my first restaurant manager.

This guy was a customer of mine when I still worked out of my second trailer. He was one of those guys who moved from restaurant to restaurant in the area. I later learned he wasn't an honorable guy. We were talking one day and I asked him, "You don't happen to have a beef recipe, do you?" He said, "Oh yeah, I've got a good one. Why?" I told him my plan was to build a restaurant building and I needed a beef recipe. I improved that recipe over time, adding more spices, but his recipe was good. I hired him when we built our first building in Villa Park and he actually was the first manager I ever hired. He cooked the beef, managed the restaurant, and helped take some of the workload off my shoulders.

He also stole from me.

How did I find out?

I had a different cash register in my first building from the one I had in the hot dog stand. It was a red register from the National Register Company. There were two key numbers on the register that allowed a person to clear the daily sales. I gave one key to him as the restaurant manager that allowed him to balance the cash drawer each night. But he didn't know I had a key for the second way to clear the register. When I looked at the balance sheet each morning, my number and his number didn't match.

I discovered he was pocketing $25 to $50 a day. That was around $350 a week—it wasn't much but it added up. I knew he was doing it, but, in my mind, I figured it was worth it to learn everything I needed to know about his beef recipe. I figured I'd have to pay somebody for a beef recipe, right? I made sure both Sharon and I knew how to make the recipe perfectly.

One day, I finally asked him if I was doing it correctly.

He answered, "Yes, Mr. P. You've been doing it for a week and you are doing it really good. This is everything you need to know, there's nothing else to learn." I said, "Good. Now you are fired. Get the hell out of here. You have been stealing from me."

He was stunned and asked, "What are you talking about?" I showed him the ledger.

He just laughed and he left. I never saw him again. I was asked why I didn't press charges, but I didn't have time for all that. I wanted to work. I wanted to get things done because I was on a roll. I had a good beef recipe, I felt good about myself, was full of confidence and the business was expanding.

It also was around this time that Sharon and I purchased our first house. It didn't have the white picket fence that Sharon had dreamed of when we were first married, but it was still a home. Our home. Our first home cost $17,000, and we needed a 10 percent down payment. My dad lent us the money. I remember he charged us interest too, but that was fine.

Sharon and I had come such a long way since I used our $1,100 life savings on a hot dog stand. And those early years were so difficult. Bill collectors knocked on the back door of the hot dog stand and asked for payments on supplies. There were so many times I think an ordinary guy would have thrown in the towel. But I kept trying to figure out a way to make the business work. I thought it had potential, even during that first day we opened and Sharon said, "Dick, we've got to close this place, this is embarrassing" because the hot dogs were so bad.

I also had my first office in the basement of the Glendale Heights restaurant. I had one desk, one filing cabinet and one employee. She was my first secretary, who actually started in my second trailer— Glenda Knippen. Glenda remained with me over the years and is the benefits manager at Portillo's Hot Dogs, Inc. Many of my employees worked for me 20, 30, some even more than 45 years. Our turnover rate was a fraction of the average turnover rate in the restaurant industry. I joked it was because I was a warm and fuzzy guy, but I respected my employees and I think they respected me.

By the early 1970s, I had three places: two in Villa Park and one in Glendale Heights. One of the buildings in Villa Park, on St. Charles Road, started as a competitor called Franksville. It was a cute building with twin roofs. When that business opened, it had a lot of money behind it and did a lot of advertising in the newspaper. Word was it planned to open around the country. At the time, I thought, "Oh god, this is terrible. The competition is coming in." All it sold was hot dogs, but different kinds like chili dogs and sauerkraut dogs. It was in the middle of an afternoon summer and I walked into the restaurant around 3:00 PM and it was a slow day. There was one customer—a businessman who had his suit jacket off and his tie undone—and me.

There were two kids working behind the counter and a 19- or 20-year-old running the place when I walked in. They made the food behind the counter and passed it over to the customer, much like a McDonald's but on a much smaller scale. I could tell the two kids behind the counter were goofing off because a couple of the tables in the restaurant were dirty. The businessman was at the counter and he asked about his chili dog. The kids behind the counter made the chili dog, wrapped it, and threw it toward their manager at the counter. Well, he missed it and the chili dog hit the customer. I thought it was great because I knew this business wasn't going to last. And it eventually closed.

When I heard their building on St. Charles Road was going up for rent, a friend of mine, Lee Daniels, my first attorney who later became speaker of the Illinois House of Representatives, went with me to the business' headquarters in downtown Chicago. The guy we met with was a tough, no-nonsense guy who had a really nice office and was flanked by all these guys in suits.

He said to me, "Mr. Portillo, I understand you started with a hot dog stand with no running water, no bathrooms, is that right?" I said, "Yes, sir." He said, "Now you're taking over my place? We have millions of dollars in advertisement and money behind us, and we're closing?" "Yes, sir," I said. He asked, "Why do you suppose that is?" I said, "You have too many guys like this around you," as I pointed toward the men in suits.

I took over the building and paid $500 monthly rent. It was probably the stupidest thing I ever did, but I was so excited because I had restaurant No. 3. I didn't change the setup one bit because I was so excited. I used their equipment, their system—all I did was put up a sign in the window that said, "Now open, Portillo's." I should have put an asterisk on that sign because our grand opening for that restaurant was one for the history books:

Don't do anything until you are ready.

I had advertised in the local paper *The Highlighter* that included a "buy one, get one free" grand opening special. Sharon and I were at the restaurant along with a guy named Paul Polatika, whom I wanted to be the future restaurant manager, a young girl (who eventually became his wife) and a high school dropout I had hired. I explained to Paul that I wanted the young kid to get used to Paul giving him orders. Paul and I made the sandwiches and hot dogs, the kid was on the French fries, and we had multi-mixers for the drinks. We made the food and passed it to Sharon at the counter. We had these metal numbers that customers grabbed when they walked into the restaurant. We would take their order, then their number. We had so many customers in the restaurant that we ran out of numbers. People were lined out the door. We couldn't have squeezed another human being in that restaurant.

We were busier than hell and Paul's face was flushed. He had a temper on him and he was yelling at the kid, who was a nervous wreck. He was so shook up he didn't know what he was doing. Instead of placing the frozen French fries into the fryer, he just placed them under the warming lights. Paul was on the beef sandwiches. What we did to keep the sandwiches moist was to dip an end into a pan of hot juice. While Paul yelled at the poor kid, I noticed his left hand was in the pan of juice. I said, "Paul, isn't that hot?" He looked down and saw the burners were off. We were selling cold food and didn't even realize it! It was so screwed up because we didn't have a system.

As if that wasn't enough, the young girl who helped us had long hair and her hair got caught in the multi-mixer. She's screaming, the customers were laughing, and nobody had any idea what was going on. Sharon was the only one with a cool head. Paul and I just sat on the floor, looked at each other and started laughing. We couldn't help it. It was utter chaos. That poor kid quit the same day. We lost so much business that day; some customers didn't come back for six months, that's how disorganized we were. I was so excited and anxious to get into that restaurant, and look what happened. Disaster.

I came out a winner on the building's lease, though.

I leased the building and land from the bank that brokered the finances. I received a letter from the bank indicating that, as the land-lord, it wanted to build a bank on the back of the property that I didn't use. I called Lee and asked him if my lease was stronger than their purchase. I wanted to make sure the bank couldn't put a bank on the back of the property unless I agreed to it. Lee told me I was absolutely correct. No bank unless I okayed it.

The bank sent out a low-level employee and I promised the bank would receive my monthly check on time because it owned the land. But I leased the property and I politely explained a bank wasn't welcomed. The next visitor was the president of the bank and he said, "Alright, you've got me by the balls, Mr. Portillo." I politely told him too I didn't want a bank on the property. He asked me what I wanted to make it happen. I think I had 10 to 12 years on the lease and I said, "Let's drop the monthly rent from $500 to $100 and the bank pays the taxes." He repeated my request and said, "You son of a gun." I smiled and told him he could call me whatever he wanted, but that was the deal. He agreed.

That meant I was paying the same monthly rent for this building that I paid on my first trailer, and the business was better!

Today I have a sign on my desk that reads, WHEN YOU HAVE SOMEONE BY THE BALLS, THEIR HEARTS AND MINDS WILL FOLLOW.

Funny how life has a way of coming full circle.

I sold my first building, that 6' x 12' trailer, in 1967–68 to a guy named Lenny. Years later in Florida, I bumped into Lenny again. What are the odds?

Lenny was living in Lansing, Illinois, when he bought my trailer for $750. But The Dog House didn't bring Lenny the same luck it brought me. He tried to sell hot dogs but he went out of business. Lenny then sold the trailer to a guy in Calumet City, and he went out of business, too. That guy turned around and donated the building to the Calumet Memorial Park District. It was a cute building but it was run down by this point. It wasn't built to last forever. Still, it didn't deserve its fate after all those years of faithful service:

Some kids torched it.

I sold the second trailer to a guy who built some additions on it, including a bathroom, though he kept the painted dog bones on the building. He sold it to another guy who turned it into the Happy House Hot Dog Stand on East Roosevelt Road in West Chicago. I visited the hot dog stand and said to the guy, "That's an interesting-looking trailer you have there." He said, "Yes, it is. It's Dick Portillo's first trailer." I said, "No, it's not." I asked who told him it was Portillo's first hot dog stand, and he said it was the gentleman who sold the trailer to him. I introduced myself and gave the guy my card. The guy said, "Holy cow. The guy told me it was your first trailer."

The guy also added a bathroom to the trailer, which ruined the "lines" of the building. He said he had to add the bathroom, but I smiled and reminded him I did okay without one. It has been a long time since I have been out there, but I have gone a few times to look at the building.

To imagine what I built from those two trailers is mind-boggling.

7

Building an Organization

By 1974, Portillo's was a success, at least from the outside looking in.

I had built my hot dog business from a trailer in Villa Park into five restaurants across the Chicago suburbs of Glendale Heights, Elmhurst, Addison, and Bolingbrook. I was making money and customers liked my food. But it wasn't all laughs and smiles. My plan wasn't working. The venture had grown too big for me to manage solo. I did so much by myself that I was being spread as thin as a slice of beef.

I had five restaurants across a 30-mile radius without anyone serving in the role between me and the manager. Many nights I slept on the work table where we sliced the beef in the back room of the Bolingbrook restaurant. I had a plumber put in a makeshift shower and nailed a small mirror to the wall in the basement. It had reached a point where I couldn't squeeze in another hour in a 24-hour day, no matter how hard I tried to make that happen. I realized I had to build an organization and hire people who truly understood the culture I wanted to implement at Portillo's.

There's an old saying that "A goal without a plan is only a wish," and I needed a plan.

My experience in the Marine Corps helped shape my mindset about organization, systems, and teamwork. I was 17 years old and seven days out of high school when I joined the Marines and was shipped to San Diego. We had 75 guys in our platoon from all 50 states and nobody knew each other. We were like a bunch of cattle going in different directions when we first marched together. By the end of boot camp 14 weeks later, 75 guys moved in unison. To me, that was amazing because I knew how disorganized we were when we arrived at boot camp, compared to what we had accomplished together by the end of it.

We accomplished it through, training, training, training and being able to make decisions under stress. That's how the restaurant business works, too. When somebody asked me what I learned from my three years in the Marines, it was an easy answer. I learned the value of organization, the value of teamwork and the value of training. I was determined to give my customers quality, service, attitude, and cleanliness (Q.S.A.C) and a unique experience—that is what I called my secret sauce. I realized I had to carry those lessons I learned in the Marine Corps into Portillo's if I wanted to reach my goals. That approach and secret sauce eventually led to what I called my four pillars of success that entailed quality, service, attitude, and cleanliness. It was a gradual process that didn't happen overnight.

I was expanding Portillo's in the early 1970s but it felt I was running in place. One night, I found myself at home watching a documentary on Henry Ford. In 1913, Ford installed the first moving assembly line for the mass production of an automobile. The show said that Ford's innovation reduced the time it took to build a car from more than 12 hours to two hours and 30 minutes. Ford's idea transformed manufacturing and society. Workers along the assembly line were taught basic steps and skills to ensure the car kept moving as it was being built. One worker did this, another worker did that. I thought, "Well, this is good," and I became a systems junkie. I thought I could follow the assembly line's strategy, as well as implement my own tweaks, and that approach would work at Portillo's.

It has.

I was a hard worker but I realized that I wasn't going to get where I wanted to go alone. Not with five restaurants, a wife and three young boys at home, all by the age of 35. I needed to have a culture and train employees to follow what I wanted and share it with other employees. It was a slow process. I spent an enormous amount of time on training, but the more I did it, the easier it got. It was an ongoing conversation that continues today because you have to have systems, training, and procedures to efficiently handle the volume of business daily at a Portillo's.

I have had a number of talented and dedicated employees who have been with me a long time. We have had so many employees who have been with me 10, 20, 30 and 40 years. If that employee was a sandwich maker or a cashier and they were with Portillo's for 10 years, they were rewarded with a gold pin and a dinner. If an employee reached 20 years, they received a Caribbean cruise. If an employee was in charge of a department, a supervisor of some kind and they were with Portillo's for 20 years, I paid for a first-class trip anywhere in the world for that person and his or her family. Employees are the foundation of Portillo's. I always felt strongly about the people who worked for me. I always did. I always tried to treat them good, but at the same time not foolishly because I had a business to run. My approach really worked; treat good people with respect and treat them decently.

Among the folks who I have counted on over the years include Glenda Knippen, who has been at my side for 50 years; Nancy Parra (30 years/Portillo's payroll); Karen Peterson (30 years/was Portillo's CFO but now is managing director of family office); Patty Sullivan (17 years/chief administrative officer at my family office); Maria Reichl (director of operations); Patti Alumbaugh (supervisor/ market manager); Tom McGregory (supervisor/market manager); Sherri Abruscato, who is in her 40th year with Portillo's, started when she was only 15 years old (she lied about her age) and worked her way up to COO; Susan Shelton (20 years/Portillo's general counsel. Before that, Susan was with the law firm that represented me 10 years prior, so you might say she's been involved with Portillo's for 30 years); Debbie Grumbos; and my son Michael, who has been with Portillo's for 40-plus years.

When I look back on the thousands of people I've had the privilege of knowing, two stand out among those who I respect and treasure the most. Patty Sullivan and Karen Peterson are people for whom I can humbly say I would have had a hard time succeeding without. Each with their own unique set of talents and expertise, they complement my work ethic and dedication to doing things right. Over the years I have entrusted them to partner with me in achieving some pretty wonderful things. They were with me during many stressful years of growth and prosperity that turned Portillo's into a world-class operation.

After selling the business to Berkshire Partners, we decided to continue on together but focus our attention in a new direction. To transition from managing the daily activity at Portillo's to embarking into unchartered territory of launching a new business, Patty, Karen, and I needed to educate ourselves and acquire a new kind of expertise. We learned to perfect this new system and created a pretty profitable environment.

Throughout every adventure we've shared, Patty and Karen have been valued members of my team. They have never caused me to doubt or question their dedication or ability and, as such, they have never been anything but amazing partners in my life's work. They have grown with me and learned from me, as I have from them. I am thankful we have them as part of my team.

Karen Peterson, who has managed my corporate finances for over 31 years, is one of my most trusted advisors. She took the job managing the books in 1986 and was the fourth person to join the original office staff, next to Glenda Knippen, who at the time of this publication had been working with the Portillo Restaurant Group for 50 years. When I owned the company, there were 70 employees in the corporate office.

I remember first meeting Karen when she worked at the accounting firm who just happened to have its business on the floor below my office at 240 East Lake Street in Addison. At the time Karen was a house accountant assigned to the Portillo's account—she oversaw everything. She knew every detail about my account and would answer all of my questions without hesitation. After a while, I questioned why I was paying a middle man when I could go straight to Karen and simply hire her as a full-time employee. So, I did.

Imagine the risk that Karen took, quitting her steady-eddy job to work for a restaurant that she scarcely knew would have the chops to succeed. When she finally agreed to take the job and came upstairs, I didn't quite know how to prepare for her arrival. That very first day she nervously looked around the dimly lit and minimally furnished office and waited for me to tell her where she could put down her box of stuff. "Oh, you need a desk?" I embarrassingly questioned. My god, it didn't even occur to me that I would actually need a desk for an accountant to do her job, let alone a real office. I walked over to the beat-up, old metal bomber desk that I used when I wasn't working at the restaurant and shyly said, "Here you go, use mine." I cleared off the mess of papers into my arms and pulled out the chair.

Without hesitation Karen sat down, took out a green-and-white ledger and started doing what she does best. She has been doing a fine job of it ever since. As Portillo's broke out of that dingy little room with second-hand furnishings, Karen did too. As I learned about the minutia of growing a world class business, Karen learned how to manage the finances. Just like the company that started so small and unassuming, she advanced to the level of expertise that no one knew she could achieve. Her financial savvy proved to be integral to Portillo's bottom line. Portillo's grew into a finely tuned instrument of efficiency thanks in part to Karen's mastery of keeping the books.

After years of dedicated service to Portillo's, Karen made the decision to retire from full-time corporate accounting just about the time I left to open my family office. It was a natural progression for her to move from the established corporation to my new family office as she was so familiar with my history, finances, and management style.

Once settled together we made the professional shift from overseeing a seasoned restaurant group to establishing a budding real estate investment and development corporation.

I rely on her to understand the financial ramifications of my decisions and expect her counsel to be accurate. I base my sometimes million-dollar decisions on her research. She can take every facet of each investment and advise me as to its value. How far we have come from that first day when I hired her to tally debits and credits and keep the books! There was no crystal ball foretelling the future of where that rinky-dink accounting job would take her, but she had faith in me and now I can repay the favor and say that she is one of the few people on the plant that I truly have faith in. I can offer Karen a much better desk today and hopefully she can agree that her office has a much better view.

Patty Sullivan, who started in 2001, began her long career with Portillo's at the front desk greeting visitors and answering phones. With her uncanny ability to manage and oversee complex projects, it didn't take but a few months before she was promoted to the operations department and then became my personal executive assistant. For 17 years, Patty has organized most every aspect of my complicated life. When I sold the company, the one employee that I required Berkshire to allow me to take with me was Patty. Like Karen, I was thrilled that she was able to seamlessly transition from assisting me with running a restaurant empire to running a family office. Patty Sullivan has the fabulous ability to master any challenge put in front of her. She does scads more than keep my schedule and make sure that I am not late for appointments. She is my ambassador, advocate, and liaison. She is an integral corporate conduit between me and many people who oversee projects in the field; as well as in my house. She represents me in my absence and needs to be able to communicate articulately my intent to everyone we do business with. Her memory is like an elephant's and she is there for me like a human dictionary of filed information on past, present and future investments. I rely on her to gather vital information that I use to base my decisions on, and in all of the years that she has worked for me, she has only let me down once.

Just recently Sharon and I were on our way to the grand opening of a restaurant on an out-lot at one of my malls. It was an evening event and, as usual, Patty sent me the address and directions, as I could get lost in a paper bag. After driving an hour to our destination, Sharon and I arrived to a dark and empty unoccupied restaurant. In a panic, I called Patty and asked what was going on. She was devastated to tell me that she accidentally gave me the wrong address. Sharon and I laughed out loud, as it was truly one of the only times Patty ever literally steered us wrong. We drove an extra 30 minutes, found the grand opening, and reminded ourselves how awesome Patty is the entire length of our trip.

I always laugh at the story of when Patty, who had been working day and night to get my new office up and running, finally went downstairs to get the mail for the very first time. It was late in the afternoon and she went to the basement where the mailroom was located. Half-asleep, she walked up to the door with a big, bold "M" on it. She tried to open the door but found it locked. She pounded on the door hoping the mailman would hear her and open it. Finally, a man slowly opened the door and greeted here with a total look of surprise. With her hand firmly planted on her hip and her head sarcastically tilted to the right, she said, "My gosh, whose bright idea was it to close and lock the mail-room door? It's only 4:00 PM." "Um, ma'am," the man responded. "I think you might be a little confused. This is the men's restroom." Red-faced and embarrassed, Patty simply rolled her eyes and apologetically said, "I've been working way too hard." I don't think she ever forgot where the mailroom is again.

Patty and Karen have proven to be so valuable that they have become essential parts of this intimate and complex machine. It could hardly run without them. They can foresee what I am going to ask before I actually ask them. They know my personality and method of thinking so well that they can look at my schedule, identify the pri-orities, anticipate my thoughts, and prepare for my arrival. It's really a thing of beauty how well the three of us work together, and the best part is that we all get along socially, find joy in each other's families, and celebrate each other's triumphs. I guess it also helps that they laugh at my jokes.

Trust has always been a real issue for me. Because so many have tried to befriend me for unscrupulous reasons or because employees I have entrusted with so much have betrayed me, I find it difficult to think anyone is genuine. But Karen and Patty are different. Of the very, very few I really trust and respect, Patty and Karen are among them. Thanks to you both.

Portillo's has so many dedicated employees and I am very thank-ful. They understood what I wanted, but these folks just didn't fall from the sky and land at my doorstep. I had to sort through dozens and dozens and dozens of people to find ones I believed in and trusted.

There were some people who simply didn't understand what I wanted, or simply wouldn't do it, or looked at me with that "huh-huh" face and the moment I turned my back, the problem wasn't fixed. I needed staying power and leaders who understood the culture and believed in it, too. How can you lead people unless you know how they feel?

What do these folks have in common? They have passion. They have a desire to please the customer, a quality that sometimes lacks in many others. In the restaurant industry, a formal education is over-rated. The people who are running a certain part of the business need a formal education: the accountants, the lawyers. I am talking about the employees behind the counter. It's so simple. I don't see why other people don't realize this. Day-to-day operations are the most import-ant aspect of Portillo's. At each Portillo's, we feed a couple thousand customers daily. If things don't go right with those customers, what do the folks behind the scenes, like the accountants and the lawyers, have to do with it? It's the people behind the counter who make Portillo's successful. They are the ones who make the customer happy, not the folks in the office. I was never an office guy. I hated it. I wanted to be in the restaurants with my employees and the customers. That's why operations, teamwork and training are the backbone of the restaurant business, especially in a complex operation like Portillo's.

As a leader, I had instincts and ultimately good people around me. As I just mentioned, there are different kinds of education, too. I've always said that and believed that. I am not knocking education because I push its importance for all my grandkids. I sent two of my grandkids to Europe to study because I told them education is import-ant. But they say, "Grandpa, you never went to college." I hate when they say that, you know what I mean? I hate that because what kind of comeback do you have?

Competitors have tried to copy the Portillo's system but they can't. Competitors don't understand the Portillo's brand because it's so unique. That's why you don't see any Portillo's clones anywhere. Why wouldn't there be more people who wanted to get involved or to duplicate the highest-grossing brand of its kind in the country today? Because the Portillo's brand is too difficult to replicate, that's why. And that difficulty stems from our training. Competitors are looking for the easy answer. How do I simplify Portillo's? I wish I knew the answer. I would love to simplify it but at the same time make it complicated enough to maintain the moat that protects Portillo's and keeps the competition out.

I had great supervisors who understood the culture I wanted instilled in each of our restaurants. Our supervisors oversaw multiple restaurants as we expanded, maybe four or five restaurants each. I couldn't talk to every one of my employees or every one of my crew chiefs—we had thousands of employees across 38 Portillo's and a Barnelli's when I sold the business to Berkshire Partners in 2014. I needed to get my point across to my supervisors. That was an efficient approach and they helped carry the culture I wanted into the restaurants and shared it with the employees. If my supervisors didn't buy into what I taught and wanted, they didn't last at Portillo's.

I also believe that too much paperwork for the unit manager takes away their ability to take care of the customer properly and keep up with the Portillo's culture. Years ago, I realized managers should have an administrative assistant do the paperwork, so the manager can know what is going on and have contact with the customers.

I hired a manager in the mid-1980s at Portillo's in Downers Grove. It was a brutally hot summer day and I happened to be at the restaurant when a customer walked in. The customer was at the counter and asked for a root beer float, where you add a scoop of ice cream into a soda drink. He said, "I want a root beer float in a frosted mug." The manager answered, "Oh, we can't do that." The customer asked, "Why not? You have the mugs, don't you? You have root beer, don't you? You have the shake mix, right? Why can't I have it?" The manager said, "Well, it's not on the menu."

I was nearby, overheard the conversation and I got up. I said to the customer, "Excuse me sir. Of course, sir, we will be glad to do that. Do you want a small root beer float or a large one? And it's on me." And we made it for him. I pulled my manager aside and asked, "Why in the hell didn't you give him what he wanted? You have heard me talk about giving the customers what they want." I knew a root beer float wasn't on the menu, but we had all the ingredients. Take care of the customer, know what I mean? He asked, "What if everybody walked in and asked for a root beer float?" I said, "We'd put it on the damn menu." That was part of my "secret sauce" I mentioned earlier. Give the customers what they want, give them an experience they enjoy and appreciate. What do I mean by "experience"? To me, it means good food, fast lines, and a pleasant environment. That manager didn't understand the culture I wanted instilled in my restaurants. I fired him a week later.

You've heard it before and you will hear it again: I didn't look for a leader who read a balance sheet better than people. I wanted a leader who rolled up his sleeves, brought everyone together and got them united behind a strategy that got things done and solved problems.

Back in the early 1970s, I hired a part-time worker, a great guy, at our restaurant in Addison. He was single, lived with his mother and he had a slew of cats. I don't know how many cats he had, but it was a bunch. He loved three things in life—his mother, his cats, and his job at Portillo's. The customers absolutely loved him, too. They'd bring him gifts at Christmas and made a point to say hello. He was great with the customers, too. He was an employee who made Portillo's a better place than the competition.

I looked around to hire some smart people around me to help run the Addison restaurant. I interviewed a college graduate from a big university. I trained him as a manager and my plan was to elevate him to supervisor at some point. One day while I was at the restaurant, I asked him how it was going. He mentioned how one of the employees—the one with the cats—asked for the weekend off. I asked why, and he answered, "Because one of his stupid cats died. Can you imagine that?"

I said, "Sit down. I am going to tell you something. Maybe they didn't teach you this at college. Look at him—his life is his mother and his cats." I explained to him that not only would he give the employee the weekend off, he'd also have to work the employee's shift to better understand the culture I wanted at my restaurants. He wasn't happy and asked, "Because of the stinking cat?" I explained to him that it was about more than the cat—it was about understanding his employees and what's important to them, too.

Here's another example of a decision that ran against what I was trying to build for Portillo's. Winters in Chicago can be rough. The average temperature between December and February is 25 degrees, and that doesn't factor in the snow and wind. Portillo's has a unique method in our drive-thru that involves several employees on foot taking orders, giving change, and interacting with customers. One particular day it was brutally cold outside. We purchased special parkas and winter clothing for employees who wanted to work the drive-thru during their shift (we also gave them extra money per hour). We provided coffee, hot chocolate, and rotated the employees so they could come inside to warm up. I was at the restaurant and it was slammed, inside and in the drive-thru. A young, female employee was working outside and asked to come in for a break because she was cold. My manager, however, said no and made her remain outside, saying the restaurant was too busy for her to take a break. I found out and was pretty upset. I made him put on the winter gear and take that employee's place in the drive-thru.

I want a leader who has the ability to get into employees' minds and understand them and know what's important to them. I worked tirelessly with my employees until they knew what they were doing and what I wanted. If they screwed up, I didn't yell at them. But I did make sure they understood. How could you blame somebody for messing up in their job if they were not trained properly? You also had to remember that not everyone's the same. You can't treat everyone the same. That made it difficult, too, when it came to training.

There are times, I believe, when a bad student is a reflection of a bad teacher who was unable to connect with that student. I was never a great student, but I was a better student when a teacher took the time with me and realized I was having problems. I honestly believe my learning challenges gave me a higher level of patience with my employees when it came to training. I had a better understanding of what they were experiencing. There were times when people treated me like a piece of crap. I always remembered that to this day. There were other people who took me under their wing and talked to me with a warm tone of voice, with some caring and sincerity. That was what I tried to do with my employees.

When I hired employees from other restaurants, I liked to say they had to be "Portilloized." They had to learn the Portillo's culture and systems. Many of these people were wonderful hires who ran a good restaurant and understood food costs, labor costs, and had great ideas. My organizational chart was fairly streamlined, starting on top with me. I had a director of operations, followed by five or six supervisors who oversaw multiple restaurants, and general managers at the restaurant levels.

What I had to do was build an organization where people understood what I taught, understood the Portillo's culture, and understood what I expected from them. I spent days and nights to make sure my employees understood what I wanted. They were an extension of me at their restaurants. They were my clones.

I missed so many family events due to nonstop work in the early years. At the beginning, I was never home for dinner. But as the boys—Michael, Joe, and Tony—got older and I added help at the restaurants, I insisted our family had dinner together every day. We talked about two things: family and business. We really didn't talk baseball or football. Our topics were family and business. That was just the way the boys were brought up.

All three worked in the business at some point, though Michael was the only one who had a love for it and has remained involved.

Michael is probably the best operations guy you will ever see in the business. He's not a computer guy. He's not a paper guy. But when he walks into a Portillo's, he has the ability to take the information he sees and explain it to others so they understand his message. One person can't do it all. You have to have people around you who understand what you want, share in your vision and are able to implement what you want done. Michael has that innate ability and it's a quality that can't always be taught.

Our dinner conversations usually centered on customer complaints that day. It was like, "Oh god, we screwed up." When Joe, my middle son, was about 15 or 16 years old, we put him on hamburgers at the Addison restaurant. At that time, we cooked the hamburgers on a grill (now we put them through a broiler). Joe was very, very fast and he did a great job. One particular day we were slammed with 60 or 70 customers in line and Joe had a huge order on the grill. Joe fixed about six or seven hamburgers but he forgot an important step—he forgot to put the hamburgers in the buns. I have seen that happen before, not only with Joe. When you are a teenager and you have a long line in a small restaurant like Addison, where the customers are watching you, an employee can get shook up. At that particular family dinner, we talked about it. I asked him, "What happened, Joe?" "I just got shook up, Dad. I couldn't think straight." And I said, "Well, that's where experience comes in. You are going to make those kinds of mistakes."

We talked about being a manager and the responsibilities that job entailed. You have to understand what's going on in the entire restaurant at all hours of the day. For example, I walked into the men's room at the Woodbury, Minnesota, restaurant, where Michael worked at the time, and I noticed the mirrors were dirty, one of the stalls was out of toilet paper and the garbage can was overflowing. When I got into the car, I said to myself, "I have to tell somebody about this." I called Michael and left a voicemail. Twenty or 30 minutes later, Michael called and said, "Dad, I am sorry. We are real busy. What's going on?" I said, "Mike, look in the men's bathroom." He looked and saw the same thing I did. And this was 30 or so minutes since I had left the restaurant. That's not acceptable. As a manager, you can't just focus on the immediate issue. You have to focus on the entire restaurant or have somebody who is qualified to handle that responsibility. That's where systems and training come in. I broke up the restaurants into thirds, like a grid or zone. And employees stayed in their own zones. They didn't hang out together. The bathrooms were part of an employee's zone and they needed to be checked regularly.

Needless to say, we had unique family dinners. Maybe talking business wasn't the right thing to do. Maybe we should have talked about sports, like baseball and football. I don't know. But Portillo's was my whole life. Sharon wasn't always happy about our conversations and many times didn't understand why we only talked about business at the dinner table. But she also worked in the restaurants, helped me tremendously and knew what we wanted to accomplish.

When I had conversations with my supervisors and managers, it was, "I don't want to just tell you, 'This what I want you to do.' I want you to understand why we do this."

For example, say a customer approached a manager with a complaint in the middle of the lunch rush. The restaurant is bursting with energy, aromas, and employees are focused on their responsibilities.

But it hasn't been the easiest shift. Two employees called in sick and one of the cash registers has malfunctioned. It's like a fire drill with all the noise and commotion. Of course, none of that has to do with how much mustard you put on a hot dog, right? What happens if that customer walked up and, in front of 30 or 40 other customers, complained about his order being wrong or that he waited too long for his order? How that manager addresses that situation in that moment is extremely important because it will leave a lasting impression not only on that one customer but other customers and employees, too.

That is why I always believed the best marketing was by word of mouth. People can look in the newspaper or hear about Portillo's on the radio, but the biggest impression happens at the restaurant. There's nothing better than somebody coming up to you and saying, "Joe, I went to Portillo's and it is great." That's why it was so important to me that my employees understood the culture that I wanted instilled at Portillo's. And how they handled a customer's complaint when all eyes are on them in the middle of a packed lunch crowd was extremely important. So, what would I want my supervisors to tell the customer in this scenario? "I am sorry, sir. I will take care of it right now. I apologize for this. I am sorry."

What if the customer said, "You know, you should do better"? Well, the customer is right. Our approach is to immediately address the complaint. Because no matter what else went on at that moment, this customer is upset. I knew that customer was going to tell other customers how we handled the situation, whether our response was good or bad.

Understanding I needed to build an organization was a big step for me. It wasn't easy finding people I trusted and believed in. God, it was so difficult at times because I didn't have the experience and the knowledge in business that I have now. It was extremely frustrating at times in those early years. I, along with my son Michael, did the hiring for the managers, night managers, day managers and the rank-and-file. Traits I looked for during the interview process were fairly obvious. Did they make eye contact? Were they friendly? How were they dressed? What kind of personality did they have? What was their body language? I made my share of bad hires, too. I learned that I couldn't train a bad hire. When we were in an expansion mode, there were times when I hired a person simply to fill a slot. I knew that person, especially a young teenager in school, wasn't going to stay with the business long-term. That was part of the process, too. First impressions were important to me when I interviewed people. That's instinct. Portillo's always had a fraction of the employee turnover in the industry. It was 80 to 100 percent domestically—most restaurants turned over essentially everyone in their operation at some point. Our average turnover rate was below 50 percent.

Portillo's is a people business. I am proud of the organization we built. It's the quality employees we have attracted who helped turn Portillo's into a helluva name and brand.

Every time somebody tells me how "lucky" I am to have achieved some success, I get angry.

Seriously.

I had a life outside of the restaurant business, but it wasn't one you might expect. It wasn't a story book with a happy ending every day. Personal sacrifice was part of my day, every day. And my family sacrificed, too.

Yet, there was also a passion.

It's difficult to explain because everyone doesn't have it. Some people like what they're doing and some people love what they're doing. Give me somebody who loves what they're doing every day. And I loved what I was doing. Honestly, I loved it so much that I was depressed on Christmas, Easter, and Thanksgiving because we were closed. Few people understand that when I say it, but that's how much I enjoyed the daily grind of what we were building.

I missed birthdays, family gatherings, baptisms, and other family occasions over the years. I can never get those days back. Many people want success but are not willing to pay the price for success. That price sometimes is about making sacrifices. There were nights I slept in the back of the restaurant on a table or in a back room next to the meat slicer depending on how late I worked. I had a plumber put in a makeshift shower in the basement of the Bolingbrook restaurant. I also put a sofa in the basement and screwed a mirror into the wall. I didn't have a business permit to put in a shower and what I did was illegal. But what are you going to do?

Often that sacrifice involves family and finances. Everyone wants to sit in judgment of people and the sacrifices they make, and it looks easy to a lot of people.

It's not.

Portillo's is a very labor-intensive operation. We've got 150 to 200 people working at every restaurant. We might have 50 or 60 people on a shift. They've got to be trained correctly in a complex business. People are often looking for that "one thing" that makes Portillo's successful. If there was one thing, it would be the people. It's the people who are trained well that make the whole combination successful. It is details, small little details, that make the big picture. It's constantly looking for new ideas and new ways to get the customer excited about Portillo's. My mind never slept; I've always had three, four, five projects going on at once.

I was always looking for that something that my gut told me customers would like. It's really hard to explain. And when I saw that my ideas were working, as crazy as they were, thinking out-of-the-box, I gained more confidence in myself, and it gave me more passion. My passion and confidence grew as I watched the smiles on the customers' faces. It was like fuel that kept the fire burning.

But I couldn't—and I didn't—do it alone.

Sharon's unwavering support, positive reinforcement, and sacrifices (there's that word again) helped make Portillo's work. Sharon attended family events solo and raised our three children almost singlehandedly. She taught my children how to ride a tricycle and ride a bike—even drive a car. And missing those things is something I regret. I envy people who are able to spend time with their children when they're growing up. But I was working. I don't share those things because I'm necessarily proud of them or to get sympathy. I say them because the sacrifices weren't just mine.

Sharon did all that while also pitching in at Portillo's whenever needed. She headed to the trailer at 8:30 or 9:00 in the morning to light the steamers. I'd get there around 9:30 to start getting ready for the day. And I would work until 10:00 PM, 11:00 PM, even midnight. I really didn't have any regular hours. Sure, I had posted restaurant hours from 11:00 AM to 10:00 PM, Monday through Saturday, and noon to 7:00 PM on Sunday. But if people showed up to buy a hot dog after hours, I stayed. And I am sure there were family members and friends critical of the idea that I was rarely around. I know, in fact, that some wondered what kind of marriage we had since Sharon was always at events without me. I didn't have any balance in my life.

Sharon never complained about any of it, though. I put in some crazy hours and had some crazy ideas, but Sharon backed me at every turn. Since we had no running water in our first restaurant, I brought the dishes home each night and we washed them in the bathtub. We were probably the only people in our apartment building that had a mustard ring around the tub.

Sharon was great, a saint. That's why in every Portillo's—and pretty much in every restaurant that I now own—somewhere there's a "Dick loves Sharon" notation in an artist's rendition of a heart. It might be in the pavement near the front door or in the restaurant corner. All I know is Sharon doesn't care what the business is or what it looks like, she always looks for the "Dick loves Sharon" heart.

God help me if I ever forget.

Most people don't fully appreciate what the word sacrifice really means. Sharon and I moved with our two sons (two years old and six months old at the time) in 1963 into a run-down basement apartment two buildings over so we could save $5 a month on our rent. Five dollars a month might not sound like much, but it was a mountain of money when you start a business on your life savings of $1,100 and an equal investment from your older brother. Every penny counted regardless of the limited view outside our apartment window.

We knew nothing about business when we opened The Dog House on North Avenue in Villa Park near our apartment. We only knew that we had to work hard every day. And, believe me, it was hard work. I worked every single day for three consecutive years, closing the doors only on Easter, Thanksgiving and Christmas Day. I also got off early on Sundays.

When that is your schedule and you have no backup, you also can *never* call in sick. I remember the time I had the flu really bad. Oh god, I was so sick. But I never thought about not opening The Dog House because I was the lone employee. Somebody had to man that 6' x 12' trailer, and that somebody was me.

I was so sick and I remember it was so cold that day. The flu won. I passed out in the trailer. Hit the floor.

Somebody looked through the window and saw me laying in the trailer and called the police. I remembered waking up and seeing a policeman in his uniformed leather jacket in front of me. He repeatedly asked, "Are you okay? Are you okay?"

I told him I felt awful and decided to make an executive decision. I closed the trailer; it was the first time my little business had ever closed during what the sign said were my working hours. I didn't want to, but I had to. The flu got me that time. But I also learned when you don't have anything to fall back on, it's amazing how far and how hard you will push yourself. Sometimes you push harder than you should.

Even later when we turned that small trailer into a restaurant empire, sacrifice was part of the equation. My employees were important to me and I made sure I was generous with my time. I may have had a fancy office with fancy artwork, but I truly preferred to be at the restaurants, especially during lunch. I enjoyed being behind the line, making sandwiches and working side-by-side with others. I thrived on the energy and excitement.

It wasn't uncommon for me to return to the office midafternoon smelling of peppers and French fries. I always had time for a good joke or a good laugh, but when it came to business, I was serious. I'd drive by restaurants at all hours of the day and if there was a long line in the drive-thru or I saw a light out on the sign, I'd ask my assistant, Patty Sullivan, to get a hold of the supervisor and ask him why there were only two employees outside the drive-thru. If necessary, I'd pull over and jump right in to help.

I wanted to focus on all of my employees, in particular those on the front lines. I wanted my passion—and the passion of managers and supervisors—to become their passion. I didn't want Portillo's to be just good, I wanted it to be great. And to achieve greatness, we had to take customer service to the highest level. And to do that, the employees in the field needed to share our passion for excellence. They need to not just meet customers' expectations; they need to exceed those expectations.

You might go into a restaurant and the waiter's crawling down your throat, asking "How's the food? Is everything okay?" They have been trained to get in your face and do that. And you might know it's phony in some instances. But at Portillo's, it's not phony. I believe there is a genuineness about the people who have worked for me that is infectious, and I want to think it comes from me. My management style was to get qualified people who worked hard. But I also really cared about them and tried to go out of my way to take care of them. My goal in life is to make other people happy.

I was an absolute stickler about the quality of our food products. I would not serve something at my restaurant unless I was convinced it was the highest quality that I could find. The food we serve is really, really good and, at the end of the day, that's the most important thing, and I would do *anything* it took to make sure we never lost that edge.

While I had the ability to attract capable people, empower them to run a good organization and have enthusiasm, I also had my eyes on the smallest of details. If I walked into a restaurant and saw a dirty window, I'd take the young man or young woman who is responsible to keep that window clean and, with a squeegee and a spritzer in my hand, I'd clean that window and explain to them the way I would like them to clean it. I never stood back and instructed, I leaned in to make sure they saw the guy whose name was on the building doing it right.

I've been in their shoes. And I knew that people who saw the boss sacrifice and get dirty were more willing to do their jobs correctly.

Sacrifice obviously means you "give up something" and as I grew older and our company grew bigger I made it a point not to allow others to miss some of the things I did. I learned over the years how precious time is and how critical it is to share that time with your family when those opportunities arise.

One day I was at a party and ended up in a conversation about this with the daughter of Peter Huizenga, a neighbor of mine in Oak Brook, Illinois, and the chairman of Huizenga Capital Management. Peter's cousin, Wayne Huizenga, also a friend and the well-known businessman and entrepreneur who introduced baseball and hockey to South Florida as the first owner of MLB's Florida Marlins and the NHL's Florida Panthers. Sadly, Peter passed away in May of 2018 and Wayne passed away in March of 2018. The Huizenga family founded Waste Management.

Peter's daughter and I talked about the long hours, effort and the time Peter and Wayne had to put into their businesses to accomplish their goals. She said all those things were likely true for me too, because she knew that was the price for success. She has two young children and I told her to enjoy her children because they grow up so quickly. Before you know it, they are not babies anymore and you are going to miss that time. She told me she actually had just talked to her children about her father (and their grandfather) and his cousin and about the sacrifices each made during their careers.

As a business owner, you sacrifice so many things during your life, but look at what you are able to give your children and your grandchildren because of those sacrifices. As a parent, you have to look at it that way and hope your children see it the same. She said that's the way she looked at it as a daughter and that was the message she shared with her children, and I felt better when she told me that. And I have tried to tell my children that in a roundabout way.

I learned a difficult lesson when my son Michael played high school football. I opened my fifth restaurant in Bolingbrook in the early 1970s and over the next few years I didn't have any supervisors. I had a manager for each restaurant and one woman in the office. But if something went wrong or someone didn't show up for work, I always made myself available to pitch in.

Michael played tight end and was a pretty good football player. In 1976, his team played its rival on a Saturday and Michael tried to make it easy on me. He said, "Dad, I know you are busy. I know you're probably not going to make the game." I interrupted him and said, "No, I am going to make it. I am going to make it." He gave me that look like he had already forgiven me and said he understood if I couldn't.

So, the game was about to start and of course, I was still at the restaurant. And it was one of those days. The broiler broke down and I had a couple employees who didn't show up for work. I walked around the restaurant with the manager and I repeatedly looked at my watch. Finally, I got out of there and jumped into my car and sped the 25 miles to the high school for the game.

I pulled into the parking lot and the game was late in the first quarter. The parking lot was filled with vehicles and I finally found a space near the back of the lot. I jumped out of my car and literally ran across the parking lot to the stadium. And, as I was running, I heard the crowd's roar and "Portillo" over the public-address system.

"Shit," I thought.

When I got into the stadium, I found out Michael caught a short pass over the middle and ran 68 yards for a touchdown. It was his first career touchdown catch.

And I missed it.

Michael knew I missed it too, because he had looked up in the stands for me. And I wasn't there. That's what most players do, and that's what I did when I played high school football. I was a lineman on our Argo Community High School, Class of 1957. I looked in the stands for my parents during every game.

When I finally reached the stands for Michael's game, I yelled to him down on the sideline to let him know I was there. I don't think I ever apologized for missing his catch, but following the game I congratulated Michael. Even with his helmet on, I saw the smile through his facemask.

That meant a lot to me.

Later on, I also telephoned Michael's coaches and got the game film of his touchdown catch. At least I was able to watch it and share in the memory that way. To this day I can't tell you why I stayed that extra five minutes at our restaurant. The part of me that thinks, "God, there's always something to do to please the guests" is in my DNA. There's always something we can do to make the customer's experience better. You get caught up in what's going on at that moment when striving for perfection.

But a couple of minutes was the difference between watching a milestone accomplishment by my son in high school and hearing about it on the field's public-address system as I ran across the parking lot. That moment can never be relived "live" in my memory. Michael never had another "first" touchdown. I later saw it on video but I didn't see it in real time.

Even now, when I think of that moment, tears come to my eyes. That moment is gone.

There was an instance when one of our restaurant managers wasn't himself, wasn't on his game. He was a great manager and a hard worker who believed in and ensured our golden rules of quality, service, attitude, and cleanliness were being enforced. But I could tell he wasn't himself during a busy lunch push. I found out his son was in a hockey accident and in a California hospital. I told him he needed to be with his son—not at the restaurant—and I would charter a plane for him if that helped.

He was with his son the next day.

Sharon and I have three children, all boys—Michael, Joe, and Tony.

Michael followed in my footsteps working at Portillo's. He has my instincts for the business and he really, really likes the business. I know he's my son, but there's nobody that knows the operational side of Portillo's like Michael. He is that good.

Joe and Tony were involved in the business early on, but it wasn't their passion. Joe was a darn good basketball player and he was the fastest kid I ever met. I still think he holds the 100-yard dash record at the junior high school he attended. I know he was fast because I could never catch him when he did something wrong. I think if he was two or three inches taller, he could have played college and professional basketball. He was that good. He had the moves, the instincts.

Tony was a great athlete, too. He really enjoyed BMX racing. He had a roomful of trophies and was ranked third in the world and number one nationally in his age group at one time. He recently earned a black belt in karate. And I respect that because of the discipline that it took for him to do accomplish that.

I can't tell you how many times I was out with the boys and somebody said to them, "Don't you want to be like your father when you grow up?" Oh, I hated when they said that. It just broke my heart. Each of my sons is his own person. Each one's different. My good fortune is that, unlike Joe and Tony, Michael actually really enjoyed the business.

Maybe I'm looking for excitement in my life all the time. I always try to do a self-inventory. Am I crazy? Am I goofy? Am I a good guy? Am I a good parent? Am I treating people differently? Am I a jerk?

I look in the mirror and I want to see what looks back at me. I wish I would have been a better father—not that I think I was a bad father. But I wish I would've spent more time with my family. That's my only regret in life. Only one. But I was working, working, working.

So, when somebody says I'm lucky, I want to punch them. My luck was made with sacrifice and moments I will never get back. Yes, I am lucky in certain things. I love my family. I don't have to worry about the mortgage. But people don't always know the full story.

That's why I tell my supervisors and managers, "I don't care how busy we are. Your kid has a game. Your daughter has cheerleading. You will go. This guy will take your place. And you'll do the same for him." Don't pass that stuff up. It's important. Because if you do miss it, you'll be sorry later.

Sacrifice comes at a cost you can't calculate.

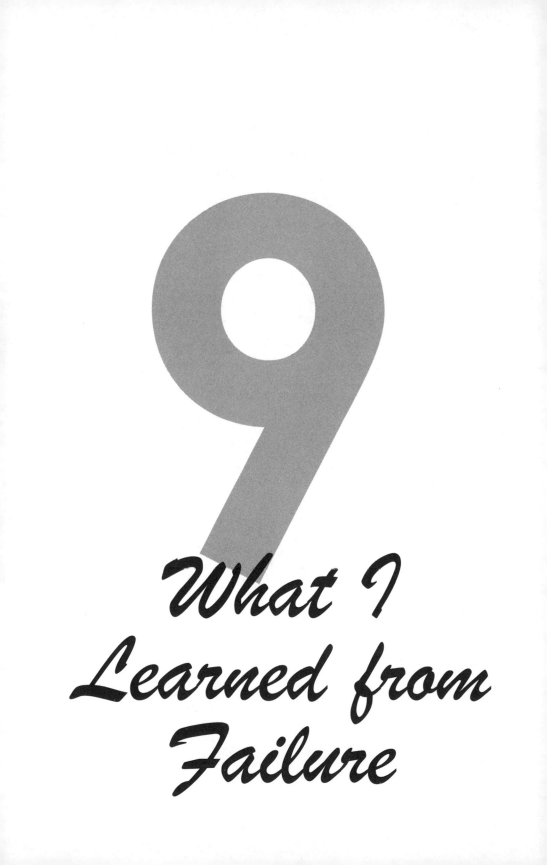

9

What I Learned from Failure

Mistakes can be the best teachers in the world.

It is easy to celebrate successes. But the truth is, I have "learned" my way through many failures as a businessman. Lord knows, I made plenty when I opened The Dog House in 1963. Sharon and I laugh at the memories. They all are close to my heart, but some are so funny they are embarrassing. I am the multi-millionaire who sold his first hot dog without ever tasting it or knowing how to steam a bun.

On August 1, 2014—the day I sold the company—I was worth over $1 billion dollars. It was a difficult road to reach that milestone. I was so dumb at times.

When I had my first building in Bolingbrook (restaurant No. 5) in 1971, somebody talked me into putting a glaze on the floor that was advertised to shine and sparkle. I brushed the glaze on and it lasted about a week or two, tops. When we mopped the floor at night, the glaze flaked up and the floor turned really slick. It was a cheap product and the company I purchased the glaze from eventually went out of business. The floor was so slick it was dangerous; I was afraid somebody would slip and fall. We spent the entire night in the building scrapping off the glaze with razor blades and sanding down the floor to be ready to open in the morning.

I also remembered one night at The Dog House in Villa Park it was raining so hard I didn't want to cross the parking lot to dump the grease down the oil bin. Instead, I dumped the piping-hot oil from the fryer down the storm sewer in the shopping center parking lot. Because of the driving rainstorm, the storm sewer started to overflow, and suddenly there was grease in the parking lot. Cars that drove through the lot near the drain started to slide when the drivers braked. There was a Walgreens in the shopping center, and the store had a lunch counter in it at the time. The city thought Walgreens was the culprit and it gave Walgreens hell. Sorry, Walgreens, I am coming clean 50-plus years later. It was me. I swear I never tossed grease down the sewer drain again.

The key to handling any kind of failure is learning something from it. It was a philosophy I've tried to follow during my career. Not everything I tried worked. As a business, you will always have complaints. We had more than 20 million transactions a year when I owned Portillo's. We had complaints, but it was how we handled those complaints that was important. That's why failures can be just as valuable as successes. That's why I was so fanatical about training, steps I learned when I was in the Marines. The value of teamwork, the value of organization, the value of training. I used those three things so much during my career. Service was my basic strategy; spoil the customer. I was determined to create my own niche where nobody could compete with me. Not only did I want to beat the competition, I wanted to intimidate it. That was my education in business. That was my formal business training. I called it Asphalt University.

Even when it's translated into Japanese.

By 1988, I had 16 locations in the Chicago area with 1,000 employees that generated millions of dollars in sales. I was the highest-volume hot dog chain per unit in the United States. Two years earlier, a group of Japanese investors had contacted Vienna Beef in Chicago. Vienna Beef has been located in Chicago since the Columbian Exposition of 1893, and its estimated revenue in 2015 was $130 million. The Japanese investors wanted to bring a unique American product to Japan to compete against McDonald's, and what's more American than the hot dog?

Before Vienna products arrived in Japan, Japanese food manufacturers had their own version of a hot dog that was made out of...fish. The Japanese's version of a hot dog was mushy and eaten cold. The Japanese investors toured the United States and studied the hot dog establishments that Vienna Beef served. When the group arrived in Chicago, Vienna Beef encouraged them to visit Portillo's.

My managers from various restaurants told me the Japanese investors were taking photographs of Portillo's, measuring inside and outside of the buildings, asking questions, and purchasing food off the menu. Jim Bodman, chairman and CEO of Vienna Beef, telephoned and said, "Dick, would you talk to some Japanese people about opening up in Japan or explaining your concept?" I answered, "What's in it for me? Why should I do it?" Bodman said, "They want to open up a hot dog business and maybe you can be involved." I never had entertained any thoughts of expanding into the Orient—all of my restaurants were in the Chicago area—but I was intrigued.

I agreed and met the Japanese investors for the first time in 1988 at my office. They were cordial and the meeting went well. Next, they invited me to Japan, and I brought along my son Michael, a restaurant supervisor and one of our assistant mangers, a blonde woman who spoke Japanese. Her parents were Dutch missionaries who worked off a Japanese island and her first language was Japanese. I thought she could be an advantage for us in negotiations because she knew their language, so I brought her with us to Japan. We also had a true translator with us that let us know what they were saying.

Remember, this was 30 years ago and in Japanese culture, men are heads of the household and women are dependent on men. We wanted to be prepared, professional and polite and were schooled on Japanese customs before we traveled to Tokyo. We had business cards made that were English on one side, and Japanese on the other. We learned how they exchanged gifts, how they shook hands and the proper etiquette in business meetings. Still, it was an uncomfortable setting for the Japanese when my female manager, who fully understood the Japanese language, sat next to me at the main table during our meeting in Japan. That simply did not happen much in that nation at the time. They asked me a number of times what her position was Portillo's. I introduced her as my "secretary" and said she was there to take notes. What the Japanese did not know at first was that she fully understood their language.

When the Japanese asked me how I picked locations for Portillo's, well, I told them. I also made sure the official translator translated it exactly how I said it. It's a story I told many times during my negotiations in the States, and it expresses how much I valued the importance of location, location, location. I saw my son Michael sink into his chair as I told the group how I picked a location: "I walk from one corner of the site to the next corner of the site, to the next corner and back to the beginning. After covering the entire area, if I didn't get aroused, I knew it was not the spot for a Portillo's."

Obviously, what I meant was I trusted my gut.

There was a moment of silence because I am sure they didn't know what to think of my explanation. Or maybe it was lost in the translation. Eventually, everyone laughed nervously. I thought it was a riot. My female manager also understood Japanese, so she was extremely helpful when the Japanese investors communicated to each other in their language during the meeting. This gave me a tremendous advantage on how they were thinking. When we'd take a break, I asked her, "What did they say?" She said, "Well, this guy over here doesn't like the idea, this guy does…" I'd come back after the breaks and addressed their concerns. They thought I was pretty brilliant!

The Japanese also couldn't pronounce "Portillo's" because they had trouble with the Ls. They instead called the restaurants "Chicago Dogs." In their dialect, they pronounced it as the "hotu dogu" business. The said to me, "You're in the hotu dogu business." I countered and said, "I am not in the hotu dogu business. I have beef, hamburgers and sausage, too!" But I couldn't get my point across to them. The older Japanese are stubborn at times. They were focused on only selling hot dogs.

We didn't reach an agreement until two weeks after that meeting in Tokyo. My terms included a percentage of gross sales for 20 years, until 2008. I also made $100,000 in consulting, all in exchange for an eight-week training course that I provided for the Japanese management of Chicago Dogs. They sent a team to Chicago and we trained them at the restaurant in Naperville. They were very good students. I stressed in training they had to be polite, and they were extremely polite. One of the gentleman took a customer's order at the restaurant and said, "Thank you very much" five or six times in succession. Everyone smiled but I said one "Thank you" was enough. We had a long line and we needed to keep people moving. But they were great students, quick learners, and hard workers.

The concept of a hot dog bun was new to the Japanese, too. They sent some of their bakers to work with Mike Marcucci of the Alpha Baking Company. Mike's a class act, a gentleman. The Japanese bakers made a great hot dog bun, probably better than what we received in the United States. They handmade their hot dog buns and they were very expensive to make. That was a huge expense. The real estate in Japan was a huge expense, too.

In 1988 in Japan, that was probably some of the most expensive dirt in the world. You couldn't own the land either. That land stayed in the name of the Japanese family that owned it. The taxes were astronomically high as well. It was a complicated issue and difficult to understand. They also did a television commercial in Tokyo that explained to residents how to eat a hot dog. They only unwrapped the hot dog partially from the wrapper.

It was a challenge from start to finish even though the Japanese promoted the heck out of the three restaurants the investors opened. They rolled out television personalities, athletes, dignitaries. They sold a ton of hot dogs, and I mean a ton. The third restaurant they opened was on the busiest corner in Tokyo, near Shibuya Station. I was told more than 120,000 people went by that corner daily to catch trains, taxis, and buses. Selling thousands of hot dogs wasn't the issue. The restaurants couldn't make enough money. The real estate was so high and space was very, very limited in Tokyo. They didn't have the space for storage at the restaurants, so the storage was a half-mile away. The cost of looking to ship the beef was astronomical because they didn't have their own commissary. I recommended opening a restaurant in the Tokyo suburbs because they already had a burger chain and a McDonald's there. But they did not have a hotu dogu restaurant.

I stressed to the Japanese investors that selling only hot dogs didn't make financial sense. If I sold just hot dogs I would not have been in position to sell 38 units of Portillo's to Berkshire Partners in 2014. Nobody has made a lot of money just selling hot dogs. Many people have made a good living, but the margins are not there. I'd rather sell something for $5 or $6 than $1.50 or $2. I told them, "Gentlemen, you will need to sell something more than hot dogs, because the margin isn't there in hot dogs in order to pay for the overhead that you are going to get from the cost of the real estate and the cost of handmaking all those buns. What are you going to charge?"

They didn't charge enough. The restaurants lasted three years.

The success of Portillo's afforded me opportunities to try other restaurant ventures. Expansion also came with hard lessons.

In 1987, I built and opened an eatery called Barney's in Bloomingdale. I opened it in a combination with Portillo's and basically had two restaurants under one roof, which was very unusual at the time. Barney's served slow-cooked barbecue ribs, chicken, sandwiches, and fresh-cut French fries. (They fried better that way and, though a little greasier, they had a really great taste.)

I got the idea for the restaurant from a place called Russell's Barbeque in Elmwood Park, Illinois. Russell's building may not look like much from the outside, but it is an institution in Chicagoland. I liked the concept, I really did, but Barney's failed. Nobody really knows why it failed, including me. I don't think I gave customers enough time to get comfortable with the concept, and the exposure probably wasn't there. The product was good, but customers were like, "What is a Barney's? We want Portillo's." That's all I heard.

I started to advertise and ran coupon specials, but the only time customers returned to Barney's was with a coupon. I wasn't making money when I continuously offered coupons. I closed Barney's because it just wasn't profitable. After I closed, customers said, "Oh, we loved it. Why did you close it?" I said, "You didn't love it enough. You didn't come back enough." I always thought, "Get rid of a bad idea, even if you think it's a good idea, if the customer thinks it's a bad idea."

I also tried my hand at pizza in 1989. Connie's Pizza is another beloved institution in Chicago, which is known for its deep-dish pizza. It was founded in the 1950s and operated by Connie DeGrazia and her husband, Ray, on Chicago's south side. Jim Stolfe traded his Oldsmobile Starfire for the freestanding storefront and he became a pioneer in pizza delivery.

Jimmy was an entrepreneur who never graduated from high school. He had a brilliant idea and sold pizzas from red checkerboard delivery trucks that drove around Chicago neighborhoods. He had 25 trucks on the road at one time, and he later sold pizzas from those trucks at Soldier Field, McCormick Place, and other local sports stadiums. People called Connie's and placed their orders and, boom, a delivery truck showed up at your door five, 10, maybe 15 minutes later. Jimmy had hot pizzas on the road even before folks ordered them, and his business went bananas. It was a brilliant idea.

Jimmy pretty much started out the same way I did. He went from job to job until he purchased Connie's. It was a small storefront restaurant with two or three tables. The building didn't have air conditioning but he had a big fan in the window above the door. Customers had to duck underneath the fan to get into the place. He made his pizzas in that building and the smell from those pizzas was so good. Like many businesses at that time, Jimmy was closed on Mondays. I visited Jimmy on a Monday afternoon and the telephone was ringing off the hook. I said, "Jimmy, why the hell don't you open the place on Monday?" He answered, "I have been thinking about it, but that's when everyone takes a day off." I said, "Rearrange the schedule, man. You are losing all this business." Jimmy eventually opened on Mondays and he told me his business increased by a quarter of a million dollars annually.

At that time, real estate was very expensive. I saw places in Bloomingdale and Schaumburg that I liked, and I ended up purchasing five or six acres in Schaumburg. That was my biggest investment at that point in my career. I approached Jimmy and said, "Why don't we put two restaurants under one roof?" He said, "What do you want to put two restaurants under one roof for?" I told him I thought the concept would work. We'd put Portillo's on one side and Connie's on the other side. In addition to pizzas, his menu included pastas and salads. We had separate kitchens, separate everything. They were separate businesses. I owned the building and the land and Jimmy paid me rent. Jimmy liked it and said, "It's a good idea." Unfortunately, this business didn't work either and only lasted about six months. Jimmy couldn't get past selling only pizza out of his mind. He really didn't put a lot of time into the pastas. Jim is one of the greatest guys I've ever met. I love him and his family.

When Jimmy moved out, I leased the other part of the property to a bridal suite. The company only had a few employees and we shared parking. That situation worked out well. Still, I really thought the idea to incorporate Portillo's and Connie's Pizza under one roof was a great idea. It was idea that didn't work, but it was an offshoot to the Barnelli's Pasta Bowl concept that I introduced in 1993 in Portillo's. Barnelli's features a variety of pastas with homemade sauces, gourmet salads and hand-tossed pizzas. It first opened in my Schaumburg restaurant and has additional locations in Naperville, Vernon Hills, Glendale Heights, Niles, Summit, Crystal Lake, Chicago, and Willowbrook.

In the late 1970s, I started to take my family on the first of many trips to Key West, Florida. I loved the community's quaint shops, seafood restaurants and laid-back atmosphere. I always wanted to bring that type of experience to a restaurant to Illinois. It took two decades to realize that dream, but I opened a Key Wester Fish & Pasta House in 1996 in Naperville. (I had already opened a Key Wester in Naples, Florida, a year earlier.) I put in a 2,200-gallon fish tank that had live coral reef and tropical fish in it and served as a room divider. The bar inside the 15,000-square-foot restaurant was called Hemmingway's and I gathered many of the artifacts inside the restaurant myself.

The menu included a selection of fish that was flown in fresh from Florida. We had shrimp, scallops, crab cakes and Key Lime pie that was made fresh daily. I put my heart and soul into that restaurant.

But while my heart and soul was in it, I also made a terrific mistake, one I learned from in a big way. My dream for the Key Wester was that it would grow as a group of restaurants. Both restaurants were big, with about 500 seats in each. The restaurants were full service, which was a shift from the "fast casual" model that had made me successful.

My first big mistake was that I tried to run the Key Wester restaurants the same way I was running Portillo's…and with the same people. I had comfort with those people, but it was an error to think that all their skills were transferable to what was, in truth, a different ballgame. In hindsight, I should have gone out and hired people who understood the full-service business to give us the best chance at success.

It might seem overly simplistic to say those choices—building the restaurants too big and then not hiring staff with experience in that piece of the business—led to the failure of the Key Wester brand, but I take full responsibility for taking a good idea and not delivering on its potential.

Sales started to drop and costs started to rise. In an effort to save the idea, I tweaked the menu to include more affordable items, but we continued to hemorrhage money. It was a very emotional and difficult decision for me, one that I didn't take lightly. But it was one I had to make as a businessman.

I closed Key Wester in 2011.

Portillo's Home Kitchen is the restaurant group's catering and shipping division. It has really grown into a lucrative business for Portillo's: catering sales earned $28 million annually, shipping $4 million annually. It offers a wide range of products, including Portillo's famous Italian beef, fresh pasta trays, gourmet salads, and barbecue ribs. Boxes of Italian beef, hot dogs, ribs, and tamales are available for shipping to all 50 states.

The catering business takes planning and organization. I found out the hard way what happens when you are not prepared to open a catering business.

I had several restaurants under my belt and the business was rolling in the early 1980s. One morning I was out running with a group of people when a guy who was a local banker asked me if I still dealt with the company that was cooking my beef. I said, "Yeah, why?" The guy told me he heard at his bank the business was closing because it was behind on its mortgage on its commissary. I stopped in my tracks and told the banker, "Wait a minute, please don't do that. You will put me out of business. I will work on something, don't do it."

I ended up buying the company which also had a catering business and I paid off all of their bills. Now I had a catering business and a commissary. We designed a special catering menu for beef, peppers, salads, hot dogs, etc. Our restaurant in Arlington Heights, which opened in 1986, was next to the Motorola office and plant. Motorola scheduled its Christmas party with us, and Motorola had hundreds and hundreds of employees. We were scheduled to cater their party at 11:00 AM and the deal was worth thousands of dollars to us.

It happened to be an extremely cold winter. We didn't have a garage for trucks we leased from the former owners of the catering business that were scheduled to deliver the food to Motorola. I said, "Let's run the trucks all night because it's supposed to be 15 degrees below zero." That morning, my telephone at the office started to ring. It was the Christmas holidays and we were busier than heck. The one call that ruined my Christmas spirit was being told the catering trucks wouldn't start (they weren't left running all night like I had asked). It was a mess. We delivered the food two hours late but by that time, Motorola was so pissed they allowed everyone to go home. We ruined their Christmas party and they let me know it. Motorola employees didn't return to Portillo's for years.

The entire episode provided a valuable learning lesson: my future can't be in someone else's hands.

There also was a time when I wanted to open a restaurant in Rolling Meadows, a suburb northwest of Chicago. There was a restaurant there called Big Kahuna's that went out of business. I really loved the location. All I had at the time was Portillo's and I wanted to put something unique in that location. I thought I'd partner with Chicago's Rich Melman, a restaurateur and founder of Lettuce Entertain You Enterprises. Rich, God bless him, believes in the business concept of partnerships; in 2017, he had 67 working partners. Rich and I are friends today. In those early days, however, I knew who Rich was and he knew who I was, that was about the extent of it. Rich and I met at the location in Rolling Meadows and he really liked the idea. What he didn't like was the suburbs. I said, "Why not? There's a lot of action in the suburbs." Rich said, "No, no. Help isn't easy to get in the suburbs." The timing wasn't right then but now some of Rich's best business units are in the suburbs. Rich is one of the best businessmen I've ever met, a true gentleman and a class act.

To be successful, you have to realize that failure will be a constant companion.

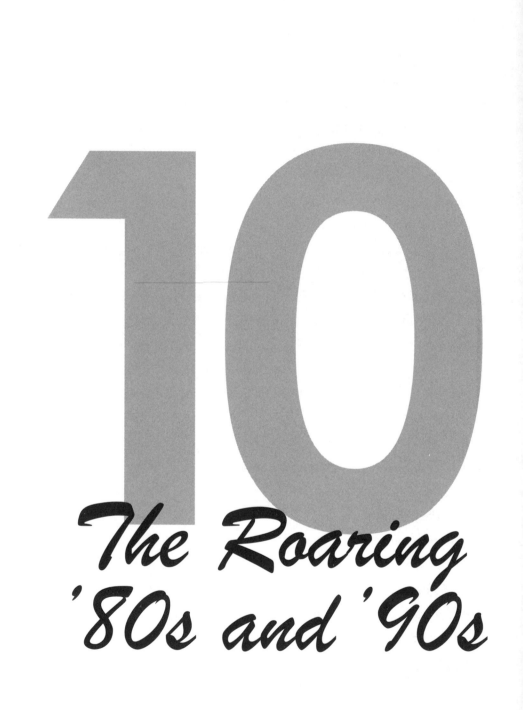

10

The Roaring '80s and '90s

A lot happened during the roaring 1980s and 1990s in Chicago, from the Bears winning Super Bowl XX in 1986 to the Chicago Bulls capturing their sixth NBA championship in eight years in 1998.

It also was a great time for Portillo's.

When I saw that my ideas were working in my restaurants, my excitement grew. The feel, smell, look and sounds of the Portillo's experience resonated with customers. From our large-theme buildings to the way I built the line to enhance the view of food preparation and the unique sound when the salads are tossed in front the customers, everything we did just seemed to click.

We enjoyed our largest period of growth during the '80s and '90s as 17 restaurants opened, including our first store in downtown Chicago at the intersection of Clark and Ontario streets. At the end of 1999, there were 22 restaurants that generated millions of dollars a year in profit. Considering I opened seven restaurants (that includes The Dog House trailer) from our inception in 1963 to our Northlake location in 1976, the next two decades were simply incredible. These are some of our highlights from the years that served as such an important catalyst for Portillo's:

In 1983, the first Portillo's drive-thru opened in Downers Grove. Almost immediately we became known for our speedy drive-thru service. I started the use of placing order-takers outside with headsets. This allowed orders to get into the kitchen more quickly and kept the lines moving at a faster clip.

In 1985, I was featured in *Forbes* magazine as an "Up and Comer" for leading Portillo's to success in the Chicagoland area.

In 1987, I opened a second restaurant under the name Barney's that specialized in BBQ.

Also in 1987 I was the recipient of the Chicago Food Service Marketing Club Hall of Fame Award.

By 1988, Portillo's was the largest hot dog chain in the Chicago area. There were more than 2,200 hot dog stands in Chicago in the late 1980s—more than Wendy's, Burger King and McDonald's combined in that area, according to Jim Bodman, Chairman and CEO of Vienna Beef.

In 1991 I was awarded Executive of the Year by the Chicago Alumni Club College of Business Administration at Southern Illinois University.

In 1993, the Barnelli's Pasta Bowl concept was introduced inside an existing Portillo's restaurant. The concept features a variety of pastas with homemade sauces, gourmet salads and hand-made sandwiches.

In 1994, after years of repeated requests from fans, Portillo's opened in Chicago at the intersection of Clark and Ontario streets. Many of the items inside the two-story store were purchased from the original Chicago Stadium, including the original Chicago Blackhawks 1938 Stanley Cup banner.

Also in 1994, I was named Entrepreneur of the Year by *Inc.* magazine.

In 1995, I opened Key Wester Fish & Pasta House, a Florida Key–themed restaurant, in Naples, Florida.

In 1996, I expanded Key Wester Fish & Pasta House in Naperville, Illinois.

Also in 1996 I was awarded the *Food Industry News'* Restaurateur of the Year Award

In 1999, Portillo's Home Kitchen Catering begins. Catering deliveries are made for the first time the following year.

More awards followed after the 80's and 90's including Manufacturer Agents for Food Service Industry Restaurateur of the Year Award in 2002, Employer of the Year award from The National Able Network and NBC 5 Chicago in 2004, the Chicago Area Entrepreneurship "Hall of Fame" award in 2006 and the "Our Stories Award" from the National Public Housing Museum in 2010.

November 10, 1981, was a milestone day for me personally. At precisely 10 minutes after 5:00 PM, I stopped smoking, cold turkey. I smoked four packs a day up until that point. It was an obsession but obviously horrible for my health. "Everything in excess" has always been my motto! I picked up running to replace smoking, and I told myself I wanted to run a marathon. And I did. In fact, I ran 10 in eight years—now my knees are shot! But that's how I approached Portillo's during our largest period of growth: full speed. When I was out running and I had an idea, I couldn't wait to get to a phone. I woke up at 5:00 AM (that still holds true today) and couldn't wait to get to work, each and every day.

When I went to work, I positioned myself in the center of everything behind the counter at Portillo's. I could see everything from that spot. I could see the customers. How long were they waiting in line? I could see the two television screens behind the counter, one of which was positioned near the drive-thru window. I could see how many cars were in line. Were the cars moving? The organization and systems I built were on display for customers, and they worked. I didn't then—and I still don't now—spend a lot of time behind a desk. I always try to better myself by being involved and interacting. I never wanted to be comfortable. When I owned Portillo's, none of my supervisors had desks. The only person who had a desk in his office was my son Michael. At that time Michael was in charge of our 12-week employee training program. His desk was in an office next to the training room. I wanted to be in the field, at the restaurants with my employees and customers. I wanted my supervisors in the field. Not behind a desk, but behind the counter, in the middle of the action.

The way I looked at it, the customer service people and the managers should be a clone of whomever is in charge. They have to go out and, if there's time, talk to the customers. You can't see what in the heck is going on if you're behind a desk filling out paperwork. Paperwork and observing the customer are two different ballgames. How do you know if the customer is getting a good experience if you are stuck behind a desk? You can't! That's why I liked being chest-deep in the action behind the counter.

That's where you truly find out what's happening in a Portillo's.

I have relied on my instincts my entire career.

For some reason I was blessed with the ability to sit across the table from somebody and immediately sense whether he was telling the truth or trying to get in my pocket. I have discovered I either like somebody right away or I won't. Maybe that stems from all the different personalities I met at a young age. And the personalities I didn't like then were reflected in the personalities of some of the people I met later. I simply don't believe what they tell me.

I relied on my instincts, from the décor in Portillo's to the items I put on the menu. I have always believed it was our responsibility at Portillo's to spoil our customers. It is more than saying, "Thank you, have a nice day." We want to spoil our customers from the moment they step into Portillo's. We are successful not because of kiddie playgrounds or toy giveaways but because we spoil our customers. How do we spoil them? We spoil them in the décor in our restaurants, the unique menu, the smells, the energy, the service. It's the whole operation that we fine-tuned in the 1980s and '90s.

Customers will see something in Portillo's they won't see in any other restaurant. If we were going to build a Portillo's in Chicago and a Portillo's in Minnesota, I didn't want the two restaurants to look the same, even if those folks in Minnesota had never seen the Portillo's in Chicago. Make the store unique for the customers. Portillo's restaurants reflect my love for history, especially Chicago history. They include memorabilia from the 1920s, '30s, '50s, and '60s. Many items I purchased myself at flea markets and other sales. Sharon would be exasperated at times, saying, "What are you going to do with that? It's junk." From the music to the décor, each restaurant has the old-time

Chicago feel that I love. But every Portillo's is unique. Each store, like a person, is different.

Every detail of the experience is important. I remember when we had the first building in Villa Park, I cooked the peppers, placed them in a pan, and covered them with tin foil. Just before we opened, I placed the peppers on the counter and peeled away the tin foil. I let the customers enjoy the smell, one that filled the entire building. I tried to hit all of those senses and it worked. As we expanded and created the Portillo's experience, a unique chain reaction was created. It's something you don't see somewhere else. You place your order and then you watch it being made in front of you as the food makes it way down a choreographed assembly line.

You can see the smiling faces of the employees making the sandwiches and filling the orders behind the glass partition/windows along the counter. You see the colors, the relish, the onions, the tomatoes, the ketchup. All this is placed in front of the customer intentionally. When we prepare the food, we do it right in front the customers. This has always been a big deal to me. When I waited in line at one of our restaurants, which I did regularly, I wanted to feel the energy, enjoy the smells, and see what the customer saw.

I wanted to feel what they felt when they walked into a Portillo's. Initially, when customers picked up their orders, our employees said, "Thank you, have a nice day." There's 15, 20, 30 people in line, and they heard the same thing over and over again. I really disliked that obligatory "Thank you, have a nice day." I said, "Let's make up rhymes. Let's have fun." Like, "Number one, you are the one. Number two, this is for you." It sounded more genuine and the customers weren't going to hear the same thing over and over.

It's the whole combination of things that make Portillo's so unique. First, we are not in the hot dog business. We are in the restaurant business. And we have hot dogs. We sell a lot of hot dogs, 60,000 to 70,000 pounds a week. But we sell over 200,000 pounds of Italian beef a week. We have two kinds of chicken sandwiches, two kinds of fish, two kinds of sausage, salads. You can go into Portillo's and eat something different every day. Americans today don't want boring. They want excitement, especially this younger generation. They want instant everything. Instant information. They want excitement, they want something that stimulates the mind all the time. Portillo's stimulates the brain. The sights, sounds, and smells I have talked about—the senses. Nobody else has that or does it as well as Portillo's. It is casual dining, but it is casual-fast. And it's unique.

Even the way we take orders and how we announce to customers their orders are ready is delightfully different. Here is a glimpse at some of Portillo's secret codes, as explained by the company on our website:

What we write: B SW

What it means: Italian beef sandwich with sweet peppers on French bread.

Alternatives: "B HOT" is an Italian beef sandwich with hot peppers and "B N/P" is an Italian beef sandwich without peppers.

What we write: E

What it means: A hot dog with everything on it. No ketchup. We call this an "ever," short for "everything."

Alternatives: If you'd like to add ketchup, that's "E+K." If you want a hot dog with only ketchup on it, that's "K—." For other combinations of ingredients, we simply write the abbreviations for those ingredients. For example, a hot dog topped only with mustard, tomato, and celery salt would be: "M+TOM+SALT—."

What we write: BC

What it means: Charbroiled chicken sandwich with lettuce, tomato, and mayo on a fresh bun.

Alternatives: If you'd like to add cheese, that's "BC+AM." Want it without mayo and with honey mustard sauce instead? That's "BC n/mayo+s." We frequently use the letter "s" to mean "sauce."

What we write: BCR HOT

What it means: Italian beef and cheddar cheese sandwich on a croissant with hot peppers.

Alternatives: "BCR SW" indicates a sandwich with sweet peppers and an "N/P" indicates one without any peppers.

What we write: LF

What it means: Large fries.

Alternatives: If you want cheese, we'll write "LF⊕." If you want your fries well done, we'll write "LF WELL."

When customers place their order, they are given a number. When they reach the end of the food line and their order is ready, our staff just doesn't yell a number and hand the customer their order and say, "Thank you, have a nice day." We make it fun and unique with lines such as, "Number 69, your order is divine," "Number 72, this is for you," "Number 81, your order is done," and "Number 68, don't be late."

The employees make it fun. As we expanded in the 1980s and '90s, my belief in my employees only intensified. They were—and are—the foundation of Portillo's. Most of our restaurants have more than 150 employees. What do they have? They have passion. They have a desire to please the customer. I have said it a hundred times—in the restaurant business, a formal education is overrated. The people who are running a certain part of that company are one thing: the accountants, the lawyers, those kind of folks. I'm talking about the people who are behind the counter. I believe it. Day-to-day operations are the most important component at Portillo's. We feed thousands of customers per day across Portillo's. If things don't go right with those couple thousand people, what does the office have to do with it? The people in the office can't help—it's the operation people, the people who are behind the counter. They're going to make those people happy. So that's why operations, teamwork, and training is the backbone of the restaurant business, especially in a complex operation like Portillo's.

It was during the 1980s and '90s when Portillo's became "top dog." I continued to scout locations, which I liked to purchase outright if I could. We served our own version of the Chicago dog, and it was often called the "garden on a bun" that featured a variety of vegetables and condiments. Our hot dogs were never grilled, deep fried, or rolled around a countertop rotisserie. When a customer ordered his Chicago dog, he moved down the line and watched employees make and dress the dog (that still happens today). We placed the hot dog in a steel flap with wheels that employees literally pushed down the counter.

The difficult aspect was the complexity of the menu. There are so many different things made in so many different ways. But I embraced that complexity. I was quoted in *Restaurants & Institutions* magazine in May of 1989 saying, "There are 256 ways to dress a Portillo's hot dog, so operationally, it can be a nightmare." That still holds true today. The structure of Portillo's hasn't changed either. It is based on a grid, with employees focusing on what they do best. Operations people, training people, legal people, construction people, maintenance people—everyone moves at once and works together. It was my background in the Marines that helped teach me the importance of organization. It was necessary to pull off the Portillo's experience. It was a labor of love for me. As sales continued to rise, many wondered if I would eventually franchise or go public. Those thoughts never crossed my mind. I didn't like that idea of franchising due to quality issues. And franchising would dilute the standards that I had set. Plus, I didn't like having to float an idea by a committee.

When I made a decision, we went with it.

The success of Portillo's allowed our family to live well and travel. One of my most memorable, and let's just say interesting, trips was to Cuba in February 1996. (I also went back in 2017, and the differences were remarkable. I thought the people were a lot friendlier in 1996.) I owned a couple of bars called Hemmingway's Bar, after novelist Ernest

Hemmingway. I had made a deal with Jack Hemingway, Ernest's son, and paid him to use the name.

At that time, you didn't have to get your passport stamped to get into Cuba. It was sort of an iffy situation; some people would say you should go, others said you shouldn't. There was a representative from Cuba in Florida who was promoting a boat marina called Marina Hemingway, so I decided to sail to Cuba from my home in Naples, Florida, with three other guys to see it. We arrived to find a really nice marina. One day, I was in my loafers, shorts, and a T-shirt, and I decided to take a shower at the marina and not on our boat for the first time during our six-day stay. I put my passport in my shorts. I wasn't in there long but when I came out—take a guess—my passport was gone.

I thought, "How stupid am I? I am from Chicago and I should know better." Making matters worse, there wasn't a U.S. embassy in Cuba. I was told the Swiss embassy could help me. A television was on in the corner as I sat there and waited. It was on CNN and President Clinton was speaking—it was dubbed in Spanish—and a video showed a fighter jet off the coast of Cuba. I asked a man next to me what was going on, and he said Cuban fighters had shot down two small airplanes over the waters north of Havana and four people on board were missing. The planes were twin-engine Cessna aircraft operated by the group "Brothers to the Rescue," a Miami-based group of Cuban exiles funded by private donations. The group had flown hundreds of missions to spot Cuban rafters attempting to flee Cuba.

I thought to myself, "Holy cow."

Finally, I got in to see the U.S. Interests Section in the Swiss Embassy. The most unfriendly person I met in all of Cuba during that trip was the American counsel. He asked me, "What the hell are you doing here?" I told him I was doing research on Ernest Hemingway, which was bull but since I had those couple of bars named after him I guess one could say I merely stretched the truth. He said, "You are trading with the enemy" and threw a piece of paper at me and said it was the trading with the enemy act. He told me if I got caught spending money in Cuba, I was guilty of trading with the enemy and that wasn't good news for me. We had a boat and I told him it was self-sufficient. The guy proceeded to tell me it would take two weeks for me to get a passport. I said, "Two weeks? Now you are going to force me to trade with the enemy." He asked me what I meant. I told him we only had enough food left for one day. I got that new passport within 24 hours, and we left before the ink was dry.

That's not the end of the story though.

We sailed from Havana and I could see the lights getting smaller and smaller on the horizon. About the time we neared Key West, we ran into a storm that is one of the worst storms I have ever been on in a boat. Our 75-foot boat was named *Perfect Lady* and I couldn't even see her bow, the storm was so bad. I was in the wheelhouse and I noticed all these green dots on the radar screen. I couldn't see anything out the windows and I asked Jimmy, our captain, what the dots were. Were they pilings in the water? About that time, the radio crackled, "Motor Yacht *Perfect Lady*, this is the U.S. Navy, please respond." "Okay, U.S. Navy, this is *Perfect Lady*, what can I do for you?" The voice on the other end of the radio asked, "Where are you coming from, sir?" He knew where we were coming from. I said, "Coming from Cuba." He responded, "Well, the storm is bad now and it's going to get worse. We would strongly recommend that you head toward safe harbor. Thank you very much."

So, those dots on the radar screen were U.S. Navy ships. I heard one of the guys on our boat say, "Throw this overboard, throw this overboard." I said, "What? Throw what overboard?" I asked if somebody had brought drugs back on the boat. I said, "I am going to rip your freaking jugular vein if there's something illegal on this boat." Thankfully, there wasn't. And besides, though we couldn't see them, the U.S. Navy sure as heck saw us and it knew the name of our boat. We didn't need to throw anything overboard, even a legal item. The boat took a heck of a beating. I told them I wanted 20 percent of everything they had in their bags! The one guy still owes me a box of cigars and a bottle of rum.

It was a great trip despite the unforeseen excitement. I loved it there.

11
California Dreaming

My parents, Frank and "Bea" Portillo.

With my sister, Carmen, and brother, Frank, at the Mother Francis Cabrini Housing Project; I'm on the left.

My parents and siblings; I'm standing in the center.

Sharon and my high school photos.

At Camp Pendleton; I'm on the right.

Corporal Portillo driving my Jeep at Camp Pendleton.

A recent front and rear view of the Mother Francis Cabrini Housing Project.

The Dog House, 1963.

Me standing in front of The Dog House, 1963.

Sharon standing in front of The Dog House, 1963.

My second trailer with an enclosure.

Moving the first trailer in the Villa Park Shopping Center.

My third building, the former Franksville. The multi-mixer mentioned in Chapter 6 sits in the background.

Sitting on the hitch of my first trailer, with my first table for four in the background. At the end of 2018, there were 18,000 seats in all units combined.

My first building in Villa Park, Illinois.

Coupons I would put on cars' windshields.

With William "The Refrigerator" Perry, and his wife, Sherry, at the Portillo's in Schaumburg, Illinois, 1992.

Recognizing my longtime employee Pauline Abruscato.

The line outside during the grand opening of the Portillo's in Scottsdale, Arizona, in February 2013. The line inside the building was just as long.

My first location in Villa Park. The post office would not give me an address, so I created 635½ North Ave. The address is still recognized today.

Surrounded by longtime Portillo's employees, with 212 years of combined service. From left to right: Karen Peterson, Glenda Knippen, Michael Portillo, Susan Shelton, and Nancy Parra.

Sharon and I toasting at the 50th anniversary of Portillo's in 2013.

Standing with Giancarlo and Tony Turano from Turano Baking Company.

With Steve Schussler, one of the most creative people I've met. Steve is a developer of a multitude of restaurant concepts, including The Boathouse and T-REX in Disney Springs and Yak & Yeti in Walt Disney World, and is the creator of the popular Rainforest Café.

Sitting with Mike Miles, advisory director for Berkshire Partners, on my right, and Josh Lutzker, managing director for Berkshire Partners.

With my assistant, Patty Sullivan.

Sharon and I in front of the Richard and Sharon Portillo Performing Arts Center at Argo High School in Summit, Illinois.

My daughter-in-law Gina Portillo and her famous chocolate cake.

With my sons Tony, Michael, and Joe.

My three granddaughters. From left to right: Kati, Niki, and Sarah.

With my great-grandson Ethan.

With Barney
Brause and
William
Faulkner on
the Solomon
Islands.

Barney Brause with Provincial Reconnaissance
Unit (PRU) in Vietnam. Inset: Barney's Vietnamese
government ID.

With Eroni
Kumana.

From top to bottom: my Gulfstream jet, my condo in Naples, my home and yacht in Naples, and aerial views of the front and back of my home in Oak Brook. Not bad for a guy who once couldn't borrow $2,500. God Bless America.

The two most important zip codes in the Portillo's story are 60181 and 90620.

The first is the zip code of Villa Park, Illinois, a suburb of Chicago where I founded my company out of a 6' x 12' trailer in the parking lot of the local shopping plaza in 1963. Remember, the post office initially wouldn't give me my own address because nobody thought I'd be around long enough to get mail!

The second is the zip code for Buena Park, California, a suburb of Los Angeles 20 miles southeast of the city. In 2005, I went out of my comfort zone—actually 1,998.6 miles out of my comfort zone—when I opened a Portillo's there.

I wasn't California dreaming, though the expansion to California was definitely a leap of faith. It represented the first time Portillo's expanded outside of Illinois. The decision to build in Buena Park wasn't made randomly. Five years earlier we started shipping to all 50 states. We had shipped food for many years on a much smaller scale, but it wasn't until 2000 when we covered every state, including Hawaii and Alaska. Many of the orders were from former Chicagoland customers who had relocated but wanted the comfort of their favorite food wherever they were. When we started looking at how that side of our business was performing, we realized that a certain zip code in California was near the top of our food mail-order destinations for several years.

So, we started there.

My business model was successful due to hard work, preparation, and planning. I lived by four simple business pillars—quality, service, attitude, and cleanliness—and Portillo's flourished because we tried to excel in those four simple things each day. We have customers who have told us they went to the original "Dog House" and continue to eat at our restaurants to this day. Their children and grandchildren have grown up on Portillo's.

We also had our share of growing pains but they were part of the process. I had decided to go "all in" on this dream of mine to make Portillo's the best casual fast-food restaurant for its customers. I had opened 17 restaurants alone during the 1980s and '90s. But I also was borrowing money, when needed, for land acquisitions and construction costs. I had never done that before. However, I wasn't borrowing money to just throw satellite restaurants everywhere across Illinois. Midwesterners know firsthand there's a hot dog stand on every corner in their part of the country. My approach was to be laser-focused— actually, make that hyper-focused—on the restaurants I had already built. I knew Portillo's was successful, but there were certain venues that were more profitable for one reason or another.

For example, when I decided to expand into Downers Grove (No. 7), the building needed to be renovated. One day, while at lunch with a contractor, I noticed a woman in the shopping center parking lot with two young children and an armful of groceries. I knew the woman wouldn't want to load the car, drive to our store, and unload her children to eat lunch. That's when I realized we needed a drive-thru lane, a first for Portillo's. I told the contractor we needed a drive-thru. He responded, "But the store's two-thirds built," and I said, "That's why we have to start right now."

We built the drive-thru but a month later I realized the drive-thru prep area was too small. It was the width of an average-sized table. I pulled the hamburgers and chicken from stations near the front of the counter, and not near the drive-thru window. I also had beef and hot dogs and one fryer. I told my son Michael, "We've got to build a bigger one," even if it was only a month old. We had space to expand, so we more than tripled the size of the prep area. Now we probably have the best drive-thru system in the country. The drive-thru was suddenly upwards of 30 to 50 percent of the business we did at some restaurants.

When we relocated the Downers Grove restaurant in 1997—we built a larger restaurant next door, 20 feet away—we never missed a day. Once we received approval from the city and the health department, we closed the old restaurant after operating hours that night and immediately started to move the stock over. I stored most of the old equipment in a warehouse, piecemealed it and used it if we could, and later sold it. But the plan worked. We closed for business one night and opened for business in the new restaurant the next morning. We also did the same thing with our Arlington Heights restaurant, which opened in 1986 and relocated in 2006. I also added on to our commissary, which stored our food and supplies and provided cooking facilities to also prepare food for sale.

The Portillo's brand was strong, and we had a loyal base and a great relationship with our guests. Even as we topped the $100 million mark in sales by 2001, we pushed forward and opened seven restaurants from November 19, 2001, to January 25, 2005. As Portillo's Hot Dogs, Inc., continued to make money, I made the decision to take a step out of my comfort zone. I guess one might say that's when I realized the Portillo's brand had legs. Long legs.

That next step in the Portillo's story was nearly 2,000 miles away in California.

I am not exactly sure when we first started to ship our food, but people were continuously calling and asking, "Hey, I really love your stuff but I live elsewhere. Would you ship to me?" It was either New Year's Eve or Christmas Eve, but one year between the hours of 11:00 AM and 4:00 PM, we earned around $1.5 million just in catering pickups in the Illinois restaurants. Not food sold at the restaurants during the day—just catering pickups. The requests from California, specifically in Orange County where Buena Park is located, arrived daily, not to mention telephone calls and emails from Chicago transplants asking us to come to California.

The California restaurant Wienerschnitzel that specializes in hot dogs and is noted for its distinctive A-frame buildings expanded into Chicago with a half-dozen restaurants in the early 1980s. But the chain, which has more than 300 stores nationally, didn't make it. That tells you how competitive the restaurant industry is. Nothing is guaranteed. Building a 200-seat Portillo's store in Buena Park wasn't cheap. It cost me around $6 million, including the cost of transporting and housing dozens of Chicago-area employees who ensured a smooth setup. It was a challenge from start to finish, to say the least.

We opened up on October 11, 2005, like a bat out of hell!

We held an invitation-only party to celebrate the opening. I relied on what might be described as "guerrilla marketing" to help spread the word. I personally went to local beauty shops and real estate offices and handed out coupons and extended invitations to the party. Who has a better gift for gab than the folks in beauty shops and the real estate industry? I knew they would tell someone and that someone would tell someone and that someone would tell someone. It worked perfectly, as around 2,000 people showed up.

We put up a large tent outside the store and a stage for actor Jim Belushi and his band The Sacred Hearts. Jim Belushi is a great guy, I have known him for years. He was from Wheaton, IL and has been a customer of Portillo's for years. I was even partners with him at Belushi's Comedy Club in Fort Myers, which has since closed. But he's such a fun guy. I was in the Bahamas on my boat with some folks, including buddy Giancarlo Turano of the Turano Baking Company, and Jim happened to be playing at Atlantis Paradise Island Resort. I called Jim and he said, "Come on over, I am putting on a show in Atlantis." I said, "Well, you know, I got too many people with me and we're leaving. But why don't we have dinner? We are across the bridge at this Italian restaurant. Why don't you join us?" Jim said, "Sure, I know where it's at." I didn't tell anyone in our group that Belushi was coming, and you should have seen their faces when he walked in and joined our table. Jim was wonderful at our California opening. He's a great performer and the people loved him. The event was invitation-only, but we pretty much let everyone who showed up inside. I also brought in a couple of busloads of Marines from Camp Pendleton for the heck of it and let them bring their families with them.

It was an incredible opening but tough, too.

The distance between Chicago and California created some logistical nightmares. Our commissary was nearly 2,000 miles away. I couldn't get a good hamburger or hot dog bun in California that satisfied me. I simply could not find the kind I liked. There were plenty of options, but the buns didn't hold up well and complement my product. That left me with one choice. I had to ship the buns from Illinois to California.

The next step was figuring out where I was going to warehouse our product. I made a deal with a local distributor in California, and we agreed on a price for storage and shipping. We needed the distribution because we couldn't keep all the supplies for a week or two in one spot. We also had no idea what the store's opening was going to be like, and we had no idea what kind of volume we were going to have that opening week. We had no previous history that we could use as a measuring stick. I know we had a warehouse full of food and supplies. Vienna Beef also had a truck that made its delivery once a week to Los Angeles from Chicago, so we piggy-backed some of our additional supplies on its truck. But it delivered just once a week so we were limited.

And we couldn't train the new employees because we had one training center, and it was back in Illinois. Very few wanted to travel to Illinois anyway, because they really didn't know Portillo's and were unsure of Chicago. I turned recruiter, going to each of our restaurants in Illinois and pulling out five or six employees and sending them to California. I had to get them there, house them, and feed them. I also had to rotate them out with other employees from Illinois, because nobody wanted to be away from home for too long. The expense was astronomical. People asked, "Well, how much do you have in your budget?" The truth was I didn't have a budget for that. How could you put a budget on something when you don't know what it's going to cost?

The budget was whatever it took to get the job done.

Leading up to our opening, the local newspaper had a story that asked readers what the whoop-de-do was about this hot dog stand coming to Buena Park. The response to the reporter's question was decisive. She said she received hundreds and hundreds of replies. When the reporter came out to interview me, she told me my name was well-known to many people in the area. I told her that was because there were a lot of Chicago transplants in California.

We knew we had a built-in customer base due to the shipping demand. As we got closer to the opening, I had my office in Oak Brook send out a letter with my name stamped on it to those people in Orange County who purchased our food by shipment. It was my invitation to them to test our food for free at the Buena Park store. We did three meals and served around 600 people at each seating.

The grand opening was crazy. The store supervisors came up to me and said, "Mr. P., we're not going to be able to make the weekend." Basically, we were on the verge of running out of food because the demand was so high. I had to fly product into a private airport and the next day we had employees on a plane with suitcases full of hamburgers. That how difficult that opening weekend was for us. It was nerve-wracking. I thought to myself, "There's got to be a way to get the supply. It was expensive as hell."

The investment in California was substantial, but I wouldn't have done it if I didn't have the confidence we could be successful there. After three profitable years in Orange County, we opened our second unit in California. Store No. 34 in the Portillo's chain is in Moreno Valley, 51 miles east of Buena Park, and it opened on March 11, 2008.

We actually opened two restaurants in the next two years between our California additions—our first store in Indiana (Merrillville, October 24, 2006) and one in Willowbrook, Illinois (October 3, 2007). I had hopes of adding additional restaurants in Southern California, but it was a daunting prospect due to the expenses and real estate challenges. Each restaurant requires almost three acres in prime shopping malls, and it's tough to find sites that big in good retail markets in Southern California.

At that point—and even though we had entertained ideas of scouting a third location in Rancho Cucamonga, located in the foothills of the San Gabriel Mountains in San Bernardino County—I didn't have plans to open any more restaurants in California.

I learned as Portillo's expanded that I also had to adapt. I wasn't going to lower my standards, not when it came to the quality of our product and the quality of our service. Why change something when you are successful?

One of the many discussions I had over the years dating back to the 1980s was with Giancarlo Turano of the Turano Baking Company and had to do with bread. As both of our businesses grew, we talked about the benefits of parbaked bread. Parbaking is a cooking technique in which a bread or dough product is partially baked and then rapidly frozen for storage. And then it is baked off at the store level.

Giancarlo told me, "Dick, sooner or later, your concept, your restaurants, you're going to start traveling. You're going to start going to other parts of the country where you're not going to be able to find the same products that we produce. So, you're going to have to find a product that will be able to travel well. The only way to do that is to have it frozen and to have it parbaked so you can finish it off at your store. And it becomes fresh. It makes for a better product."

It took Giancarlo many years to convince me that was the way to go. Initially, I purchased a full 36" or 39" loaf of French bread from Turano and cut it into six pieces and served it. Turano baked it and delivered it.

Portillo's and Turano Baking Company also started a unique partnership that probably wasn't being done anywhere else in Chicago at the time—Turano delivered fresh bread to Portillo's twice a day. It made for a better product to serve to my customers. The bread that is delivered in the morning was made maybe at midnight the night before. Originally, I served the bread for lunch and dinner, meaning it could be as long as 20 hours after the product was produced. If a restaurant doesn't have a system in place that maintains freshness, that restaurant is serving an inferior product.

And nature is nature. Bread stales, Italian breads for sure. You can't stop it, no matter what you do. You can put it in a plastic bag but that won't stop it from staling. The question is, how can I keep it as fresh as I possibly can? How do I keep it crisp? Well, you can't. If you put it in plastic, the crispness goes away. If you leave it in paper, it's going to dry out. Italian bread is not white bread. There's really no preservatives in Italian bread. There's no softeners, so the product is going to stale. Turano, the new kid on the block in the bread business, decided his company would deliver bread to Portillo's twice a day, once in the morning and once in the afternoon.

Turano was a go-getter. He had to provide better service and a better product at a reasonable cost. Portillo's had the volume that demanded twice-a-day delivery. Turano put in afternoon routes to support my business. And none of my competitors had that kind of fresh bread. My restaurants were set up to handle parbaked bread with ovens. If a restaurant is not set up for it, it becomes a bit cumbersome. I recognized it was the right thing to do. I had the space to support it and take the product. I trained my staff to be able to support the process. It was a big departure for me. But once I added it to my concept, Portillo's had fresh bread that literally traveled across Illinois and across the country. Turano offered the same product, same quality.

Bread and sandwich-making is a science. Anytime I tested a product, somebody would say, "Oh, just test the beef. Oh, just test the bread." That was fine when you want to see if it met your first specification, but it was never the final test for me. I wanted to see the entire process to make sure it was made up the way the guest will eat it. Because that's the whole experience for the guest, and that's what I always preached—the whole guest experience. I actually did a marketing campaign on how to stand and eat your beef sandwich so it didn't drip on your clothes. You should see my beef-eating pose! We used a football player in the marketing campaign.

And, as we expanded, even to California, the array of smells in Portillo's remained so important. When we were on *The Ellen DeGeneres Show* in California, we were heating up the beef to take into the studio, the gravy, to get the beef sandwiches ready. Other restaurants were on the show and nobody was allowed to identify themselves. We had no logos on our uniforms so they wouldn't know what food they were getting. And they were like, "I know that's Portillo's beef. I know it. I can smell it." I did things that helped make the guest experience more dynamic, more exciting, and more inviting. A lot of what I did was innovative. When a guest walks into Portillo's, I don't want them only thinking, "Oh, this smells great. I am smelling it; therefore, I want it." I want them to say, "I just want it."

I always strived to get people to understand the important elements of the business. What was important about the guests? What was important about how you run a restaurant? What are the things you look for? How do you make sure the team is doing things right? What are some of those pivotal points you look for, whether it is the guest interaction or the flow of the food? What characteristics do you look for? Whether it's the beef, whether it's the dogs, whether it's the hamburgers coming off the broiler. How do you set those expectations? And then how do you communicate it when employees are not meeting or reaching those expectations? Restaurants are constantly developing people.

Even though I stepped out of my comfort zone when we expanded to California, I still followed the same guidelines I had put in place to ensure the success of Portillo's. I didn't open restaurants to close them. I followed the same audit I always had. I looked at walls, baseboards, fans, décor, food safety, uniforms. Are we doing anything that would endanger the public? I engaged with customers and employees and we retrained as we went.

I was always detail-oriented. I wanted to refine every aspect of the customer experience. That's just smart business.

12

The Importance of Competition

I have been in business for a half a century.

I have learned that being an entrepreneur can take a toll on you. It is a roller coaster of emotions. Some decisions are successes, some are failures. Sometimes you feel powerful, and other times you feel like a decision has been a huge waste because of the money involved—finances, cash flow, staffing issues. Together, business can be a big risk. Being an entrepreneur can put your mind in a lot of dangers, I truly believe that.

I always wanted to be better than the competition. I studied competitors with caution. I always knew the competition was dangerous. I didn't know how to retreat, but I was never cocky. I respected the competition, but I also wanted to beat it. I want to be the best. And Portillo's was. Portillo's won so many Silver Platter Awards—the Oscars of the food industry—that we were retired over a five-year span to give others a chance. Each week, for instance, Portillo's cooks over 200,000 pounds of Italian beef a week—that's 10. 4 million pounds annually. And hot dogs—the foundation of my company—are only 12 percent of our business.

The competition hasn't figured out how to beat Portillo's.

When you look at the evolution of Portillo's, there was never a moment where I nor the company was "content." There was never a feeling of, "We made it." I always told my son Michael, "Our competition's going to close the gap. Right now, we have nicer décor, we have better buildings, and we have better quality food. Eventually, the competition is going to catch up. And we have to know that."

I always used information to my advantage. I gathered that information from our own successes and failures, and from watching our competition, and allowed it to guide me. I always looked at the type of things that made us successful. I knew in the early years I didn't have the funds to go up against the chains that I saw as my competition—McDonald's, Burger King, and Wendy's. They were corporate giants, so I purposely designed the most complicated fast-casual business in the industry to beat them. I knew I had to do something different if I was going to stay alive in this business.

It's the complexity, it's my moat, that the competition can't navigate. The competition wants to simplify things. The minute you simplify it, you lose what you have. Look at Five Guys, a fast-causal restaurant chain focused on hamburgers, hot dogs, and French fries. It opened in 1986 and started to franchise in 2003. At one time it was the fastest-growing food chain in the United States. I think Five Guys has a wonderful hamburger. But the business is not expanding anymore. Sales are down. Why? It takes too long to get your food. It's a great product but you need more than good food in the restaurant business.

You need an experience.

Knowledge is power. I always knew what was going on in the street. I was always aware of what the competition was doing. When I first opened my hot dog stand in 1963 in Villa Park, I didn't know how to cook a hot dog or steam a bun. I didn't know who sold the best buns or what the best condiments were to put on a hot dog. I had no concept of food costs. I went to other restaurants and peeked to see how they prepared and cooked their hot dogs. It was like, "Wake up. Look around." Even as I built my business over the years, many times I still went to restaurants to see what the competition was doing. I wanted to see if we could replicate something that was popular in their business and fit it into the Portillo's profile. I have always seen my restaurants as more of a special destination than other fast-casual chains. My desire was to beat the competition with quality and uniqueness.

I was among the thousands and thousands over the years who opened a hot dog stand in Chicago and the surrounding areas. I wasn't alone, but I am that one who has survived and built my 6' x 12' trailer into this billion-dollar fairy tale. My approach was different. Other businesses lived a different way and had a different approach. There are about 25 or 30 old-time Chicago Vienna hot dog stands that have been around 60, 70, 80 years. They have done very well and make perfectly good product. They have made a nice living, put their kids through college, and supported their families.

But why am I the one who has set this unprecedented standard in the restaurant business?

There are a number of empirical things I can recite. There's nothing about me that's easy. I was tough and still am. But my goal every day never wavered. I was determined to give customers an experience they didn't think was possible from this type of restaurant, and excel when it comes to value. The difficult thing was the complexity of the design of the menu. There are so many different things made in so many different ways. But we have done it flawlessly for the most part and have beat our competition. I have a list of 50 people who have owned successful fast-food Chicago restaurants who went belly up once a Portillo's opened near them.

That list includes a Pro Football Hall of Fame inductee who is one of the most marketable sports figures in Chicago with countless endorsement deals and business ventures, including restaurants, a wine label, and even a salsa.

His name is Mike Ditka.

The Chicago Bears were the toast of the town in 1985–86.

Da Bears, coached by Mike Ditka, beat the New England Patriots 46–10 in Super Bowl XX. They put together one of the greatest seasons in NFL history at 15–1, and the public couldn't get enough of them. The Bears developed a special bond with fans because it was a team that won with personality, style, and toughness.

Guys like running back Walter Payton, considered one of the greatest players all time, quarterback Jim McMahon, William "The Refrigerator" Perry, and even defensive coordinator Buddy Ryan were beloved, iconic figures. After the team's only loss to the Miami Dolphins in Week 13, players recorded "The Super Bowl Shuffle," becoming the first sports team to record a rap song. It was a huge hit, peaking at No. 41 in February 1986 on the Billboard Hot 100 chart. When the Bears beat the Patriots in the Super Bowl, it was the organization's first NFL title since 1963.

Chicago loved its Bears.

And there was Ditka. A first-round pick by the Bears out of the University of Pittsburgh in 1961, he helped revolutionize the tight end position by becoming a receiving threat rather than just a blocker. Ditka had said he hoped to coach the Bears when his playing days ended, and owner George Halas hired him in 1982. Three years later,

Ditka—known for his gum-chomping on the sideline, mustache, and aviator sunglasses—led the Bears to a Super Bowl win that helped him become one of the most marketable sports figures in Chicago.

When Ditka announced plans to open his restaurant, Ditka Dogs, near one of my best Portillo's—this one was in Naperville, west of Chicago, with a couple young men as the financial backers—I was really concerned. They were coming straight at me. I thought, "Oh boy. Ditka. Everybody in Chicago loves this guy." But I didn't know how to retreat. That wasn't my style.

Building my business model from the trailer to what it had become in the 1980s was a gradual process. How was somebody going to open a place exactly like Portillo's? Where would they train their employees? You can get all the employees you want from a McDonald's, a Burger King, or a Wendy's. But they are going to be lost working in a Portillo's-style restaurant.

They thought they figured out a way. It wasn't Mike Ditka—his name was just on the restaurant sign. But they were aggressive in their attempt to hire employees away from Portillo's. They went into my restaurants at night and talked to cashiers, the order-takers, the employees who made the sandwiches. They were in my restaurants with $100 bills in envelopes trying to entice my employees to jump to Ditka's restaurant. They asked my employees how much they made: "Ten dollars an hour? We'll give you $11 an hour if you come with us." They were trying to pick off my staff. They copied our equipment layout plan from one of my managers they hired, though they tweaked its design and it really never helped them.

My son Michael, another Portillo's supervisor, and myself set up an appointment and went and talked to them. I told them what they were doing was unethical as hell. I said I understood that business is business, but what they were doing was going to raise the cost for both businesses. I said, "Why don't you be gentlemen and do it the right way?" I told them that if they continued to try and poach my employees, I'd pay them even more money and steal them back. And this tug of war would just go back and forth and not benefit either one of us. They said, "Okay, Mr. P. We promise you, we won't take any more because we have our staff. We are good."

They lied.

They hired one of my managers at a higher salary, but I came up with a plan to get him back. It was a few days before Ditka's grand opening, and it was being advertised everywhere—television, radio, and in the newspaper. It was a full-out media blitz. I always had a good relationship with my managers and supervisors, but, you know, money does funny things to people, too.

I got in touch with the manager who left me for Ditka's and asked him if he could meet me at my home. Before we met, I stopped at the bank and withdrew a boatload of money in cash. My attorney, Susan Shelton, was with me at my home when the manager arrived. We sat at the dining room table and I told the manager there were no hard feelings and I understood he had a wife and children to support. I told him he did what every man, every leader of the house, every bread-winner, would do.

About this time, I dug into my one of my pockets and grabbed fistfuls of cash and spread it across the table. There was probably a couple thousand dollars on the table. He looked at the money and probably had no idea what the hell I was thinking. I asked him if he wanted to earn that money on the table. I told him I knew what Ditka was paying him and I wanted to know if he'd return to Portillo's for X amount of money—plus the cash on the table as a bonus. "Are you interested? Because I have more money," I said. I reached into my other pocket and tossed out more cash. I think there was $4,000 or $5,000 spread across the table.

I explained to him how he could earn all that money. He had to get the employees who Ditka's hired from us back to Portillo's—the sandwich-makers, the expeditors, the French fries guys, broiler guys, the beef guys, the hot dog guys. I didn't care what they made hourly at Ditka's, I'd pay them a dollar more an hour. I asked him what he thought of my idea. He said, "Mr. Portillo, you are a man of your word, but are you sure you'll forgive me?" I told him, "I swear I'll forgive you. What I am talking about now is important. It's business." I reached back into my pockets for the rest of the money and tossed it on the table. There was about $12,000 on the table now. I told him it was all his if he did one more thing.

He asked, "What?"

Ditka's was scheduled to open that upcoming Saturday. Shockingly, his last day was Friday.

I went into Ditka's for the grand opening that Saturday and it was utter chaos. They didn't have enough workers. Customers screamed and yelled that the food was cold; they didn't have anyone to make the sandwiches. The young financial backers—their jackets and ties off, their sleeves rolled up—attempted to help, but they didn't have any idea what they were doing. Everything was screwed up. I sat down for a cup of coffee and I could see the brothers and one of them pointed my way. I don't think they were happy with me.

I strategically responded in other ways, too. Like the time we hired a plane to fly over Soldier Field during a Bears home game with a banner that read PORTILLO'S HOT DOGS, #1 IN CHICAGO. I am not sure Mike Ditka looked up and saw the banner during the game, but the idea—and message—was a touchdown for Portillo's!

I also read somewhere that William Perry was the most popular player on the Bears. He was nicknamed "The Refrigerator" for his imposing 350-pound-plus size, and fans loved his gap-toothed, friendly smile. Shortly after Ditka's opened, I paid Perry to show up at our restaurant for a meet-and-greet. He only was supposed to be there for a couple hours, but he ended up staying longer. We had lines out the front door and into the parking lot. It was really cold that day, so I had employees hand out coffee and hot chocolate to customers in line outside. Perry stayed as long as he could and was really engaging. But he finally had to go and not everyone in line got to meet him.

A short time later, I received a letter from a young girl who said she waited in line with her family but never got in to see Perry before he left. She thanked me for the hot chocolate but said I shouldn't have advertised a meet-and-greet with Perry if not everyone could meet him.

I had booked Perry for another event at the Schaumburg restaurant, so I wrote the young girl back. I said, "I'm very sorry but I had no control over that. So, what I'll do is I'm going to send a limo for you and your family and we're going to have a table right next to William 'The Refrigerator' Perry and you will be the first one to meet him." When the limo pulled up in front of the restaurant that day, the little girl ran out and was so excited. I hugged her, shook hands with her parents, and sat them at a table next to Perry. We had hundreds of people in line but they were the first ones to meet and talk with Perry.

They stayed in touch and we talked about that day and meeting Perry for many years.

If a competitor walked into a Portillo's with the intent to steal employees, my instructions to my supervisors were, "Go to their place and put out the word that if they are going to steal, they are going to make it worse because we have a checkbook behind us." I'd go in myself and tell the manager of a competing business, "Just so you know, I am going to open the checkbook here and hire everybody. So please don't pirate." I felt if businesses wanted to share part-time employees, that's a good idea. A lot of people work two jobs. But I had an eye out for competitors that tried to poach our employees. It's hard to find labor. It's harder still to find good labor. But a competitor always knew if they hired an employee from Portillo's, they were getting talent.

Mike Ditka conceded defeat less than a year after he opened Ditka's Dogs. I guess it got so bad for him that one time during a post-game press conference following a Bears game I was told he actually asked, "Anyone out there want to buy a restaurant?" I think they lost a bunch of money on the business venture. A story in the *Los Angeles Times* years later on the challenges of the hot dog business said, "Just ask ex–Chicago Bears coach Mike Ditka, who couldn't coax Chicagoans to buy red hots at Ditka's Dogs. It closed faster than you can say 'frankfurter.'"

Ditka has stayed connected to hot dogs though. In 2014, Al's Beef leveraged its endorsement deal with Ditka with the debut of the "Spicy, Jumbo Ditka Dog" on its menu for one month in honor of July being National Hot Dog Month. Ditka also has a deal with Vienna Beef to sell Ditka Sausages at grocery stores and his restaurant chain, among other outlets.

I never met Mike Ditka. I do respect and admire his career.

I also remember the time employees of McDonald's from across the street came into the Portillo's restaurant on Ogden Avenue in Naperville, Illinois, with 15 or 16 people from Asia. I don't know if they were investors or what, but I could always tell when somebody entered the restaurant to spy. They ordered one of everything off the menu and they took a lot of notes. They were like bad shoppers. I watched this group and I had no clue what they were doing when they walked in front of the restaurant and measured the sidewalk. I said, "Okay, I've watched you guys all afternoon do this whole thing—I get you're looking for what we do. I was with you on everything until you were measuring the sidewalk. What was the purpose of measuring the sidewalk?" They said, "We want to know what makes you successful." I thought, "Are you kidding me?" I told them, "Well, this isn't it."

While measuring the sidewalks, they missed the moat that surrounded Portillo's. It was what I build that protected Portillo's from the competition. I purposely created an extremely complex design, and how does a competitor overcome that? I am a former Marine. And what I learned in the Marines carried over into my business world, the value of teamwork, the value of organization, the value of training.

Suppliers also competed for Portillo's business. I am a tough negotiator.

It was in the early days of Portillo's when in walked a jolly, personable guy named Giancarlo Turano with a bag of bread. He introduced himself and said he owned a small bakery and wanted to talk about doing business. I told Giancarlo, "Let me tell you something. I want a certain size bread, a certain diameter, a certain consistency, and color," Giancarlo said, "No problem, what size do you need?" I told him and asked when he could get the bread to me. He answered, "Tonight." Turano went back to his bakery and returned with the bread. I asked if he could deliver regularly and for his best price. We negotiated and agreed on a price that was better than what I had received from my previous bread supplier, Gonnella Baking Company. I quit ordering from Gonnella, and they became upset with me. But I didn't take it personally. It was business.

This is a story I think every businessman should know. Marshall Field, the American entrepreneur and founder of the Chicago-based department stores, Marshall Field and Company, said, "Business is simple. Give the lady what she wants. Give the man what he wants. Give the customer what they want and work with them." Competition is bad for the guy on top, but great for guys like me when I first started out. I had to think outside of the box when I first opened by hot dog stand. Gonnella Baking Company has been around since 1886 and has been an important part of the Chicago landscape for decades. Turano, founded in 1962, is now one of the largest artisan bread producers in North America.

In the years after we started doing business, when Giancarlo Turano calls me—and we are dear friends to this day—it's usually for one of two things: either he wants to go to dinner, or he's raising his bread prices. A number of years ago, he called and left a message. I knew this particular call was about raising his prices. I had my office check into the flour business. Was the cost of flour or anything related to the bakery business going up in any way, shape, or form? Were there any other trends that pointed to increased costs? I was informed prices were not escalating in any areas of the bakery business. (Remember, knowledge is power!)

I met Giancarlo and he said he had to raise prices because his costs were escalating. I answered, "So are mine, Giancarlo. Mine are going to the moon." Giancarlo said he had a lot of employees (in the hundreds), and I told him I had a lot of employees (in the thousands), too. He said the cost to do business was rising and they were constructing a new building. I told Giancarlo I didn't care about his building and told him—with a smile on my face, of course—I wasn't going to help him pay for a new building. Giancarlo explained his business had taken really good care of Portillo's, and he treated all of his clients equally. "Everyone equally?" I asked. "How many other customers order the volume of bread that I do?" He said, "Nobody."

I told Giancarlo, "If I was in your shoes and I had a customer like Portillo's, you know what I'd do?"

"What?" he asked.

"I'd find the world's best surgeon and have him surgically attach your lips to my ass," I said.

Giancarlo thought it was a great story, but said he still had to raise his prices. I told him I didn't take it personally because business is business. I told him I hoped we could still be friends, and, of course, we are to this day. Our wives are good friends, too. The meeting ended cordially, but I went back to ordering my bread from Gonnella, though I really didn't want to because I knew it wouldn't be a long-term solution. Gonnella quickly alerted the other beef stands that ordered from Turano that Gonnella had once again earned Portillo's business. Turano didn't just lose my business that day, he ended up losing many of the other beef stands, too.

It wasn't long before I got another call from Giancarlo. He was playing golf in Hilton Head, South Carolina.

Giancarlo said, "Dick, I have good news."

I asked him, "What?"

He answered, "I found a great surgeon!" Giancarlo explained that maybe I was right, and he decided against raising his prices and wanted again to do business with Portillo's. One problem: I told Giancarlo I couldn't because I had already negotiated the previous price with Gonnella. In fact, I actually fibbed to Giancarlo and told him I was getting a better price than that from Gonnella. Giancarlo said, "Okay, I will match that price." That wasn't good enough for me. I told Giancarlo he had to beat that price.

Which he did.

In the span of a few months, I had a better deal to purchase bread than I had in years. For the second time, Gonnella asked why I did what I did, but you know what? It was business. The color wasn't right and I knew it. Turano had proven again that he was hungry and passionate, and I love that combination. I believe that because of the Turano family's passion for business, they will eventually become one of the largest bakeries in the country.

The business world is competitive. Competition is good for everyone. I have two sayings that are placed prominently in my office. One is D.W.Y.S.Y.G.T.D., short for "Do what you say you're going to do." Below it, another plaque reads, WHEN YOU HAVE SOMEBODY BY THE BALLS, THEIR HEARTS AND MINDS WILL FOLLOW.

Our competition knows that both those plaques represent my defining principles.

13

Hello,
Arizona

Aside from the Midwestern states that border Illinois, it has been reported that only California and Florida outrank Arizona in the number of residents who were born in Illinois. Over the years, Portillo's was inundated with emails, letters, and telephone calls from Chicago transplants living in Arizona with one request:

Please bring Portillo's to the Grand Canyon State!

Realizing how intense our following had become by 2013, I knew Portillo's had the potential to become a national brand. The signs over the years pointed to this reality. By 2000, we started shipping to all 50 states with sales topping the $100 million mark—and the dollar signs were multiplying rapidly. A part of it was due to the popularity of hot dogs, even if they only represented 12 percent of our sales. According to *Restaurant Business* magazine in October 2003, more than 20 billion hot dogs were sold in the United States in 2002.

At that time, I had two dozen Portillo's locations, nine Barnelli's Pasta Bowls (all shared space in the same restaurant with Portillo's), two Luigi's House full-service restaurants, the Key Wester Fish & Pasta House, and our catering and shipping division, Portillo's Home Kitchen. In 2005, Portillo's expanded outside of Illinois for the first time with a restaurant in Buena Park, California. A year later, Portillo's opened its first restaurant in Indiana in Merrillville. In 2008, Portillo's opened its second restaurant in California, this one in Moreno Valley. We had built Portillo's into the Midwest's largest privately owned restaurant company, with more than 3,000 employees and $165 million in sales.

It was a great time to be a Portillo's fan. Better yet, we were more than happy to again oblige the repeated requests of residents from Arizona. On February 27, 2013, Portillo's headed west again as we opened a restaurant in Scottsdale on N.W. 90th Street and Shea Boulevard.

Our opening in Scottsdale was off the charts.

It was the biggest opening we had ever had to that point. We netted $438,000 after sales tax the opening week. I mean, that's unheard of—nearly half a million dollars! That's bigger than openings for McDonald's, Burger King, and Wendy's. We had six cash registers going and customers waited up to two hours in line. I wouldn't wait and hour and a half, two hours, for anything. But our customers were more than happy to do that. I don't remember which day this was, but during our first week my son Michael texted me, "Ended today with $82,000. $6,833 every hour, $113 every minute or $1.89 every second we were open. I'm very tired Dad, good night."

An estimated 10,000 customers showed up during restaurant hours from 10:30 AM to 10:30 PM that opening week to taste our famous Italian beef, Italian sausage, burgers, hot dogs, chicken sandwiches, specialty sales, and our renowned chocolate cake. The 8,721-square foot restaurant is adorned with 1940s, '50s, and '60s memorabilia and seats 190 guests indoors and outdoors. We had more than 200 full-time and part-time employees on the clock that week. It was wall-to-wall excitement.

More than 500 people waited in a line that snaked around the building. Our drive-thru lanes were backed up so far, we needed a traffic cop. It was a media frenzy, but the timing was right. All the snowbirds were in Arizona for the winter and spring training had started—Scottsdale is home to the San Francisco Giants, Colorado Rockies, and Arizona Diamondbacks. Honestly, the opening was so much fun. I had so many people tell me they were from Chicago and everyone had a story about Portillo's.

I felt like a rock star!

Our plan was to appeal to the thousands of Chicago transplants in the area and one of the nation's largest college enrollments nine blocks away on the Arizona State University campus. It was the perfect storm, but that was by design. I already had plans to continue our Arizona expansion with a second location in Tempe later that summer in 2013, and the excitement continued to build. That Portillo's is west of where the 2016 World Series champion Chicago Cubs' new spring training facility is located. It also is the last restaurant I opened before I sold Portillo's to Boston-based Berkshire Partners in 2014.

Chicago and the Valley are a natural fit. The local Arizona media later reported how the Cubs' new complex and Portillo's expansion to Arizona demonstrates the strong ties between the two. Another media report explained that an analysis of IRS statistics from 2005 through 2010 showed Illinois ranked in the top three states for people migrating to Arizona from 2005 to 2007, and among the top five states from 2008 to 2010.

Over those six years, an average of 12,785 Illinoisans moved to Arizona annually, more than half of them to Phoenix's Maricopa County, bringing total adjusted gross incomes of more than $260.5 million each year, the IRS data suggests. The story reported that nearly 12,000 Illinois residents relocated to Arizona in 2014—a 39 percent increase over the prior year, according to U.S. Census Bureau data.

Patty Sullivan, who served as our spokesperson, said in a published story that "I've heard it called Chicago's farthest Western suburb." Patty's right. Everyone was so excited when Portillo's landed in Arizona. The Portillo's company Facebook page received nearly 2,000 posts on its page when it initially announced its Arizona expansion.

I might be part of the Traditionalists or the Silent Generation—born 1945 or before—but that doesn't mean I am not hip to the times. When we started to install cameras in our restaurants, especially when we started expanding out of state, it was an easy way for me to check into Portillo's no matter where I was. In the early days I drove between restaurants. Fast-forward 50 years later, and one Dick Portillo learned how to use an iPad and log in into Envysion.

I was the restaurants' eye in the sky!

One time, I suffered a broken left ankle and leg in a fall outside my hotel and was in the hospital in Arizona. Still, I logged in on my iPad and as I checked on the Scottsdale restaurant. I noticed a piece of paper on the floor next to an employee's feet. I called the restaurant manager on the phone to alert him. There was the time I checked another restaurant and I saw two guests, one still waiting for her food.

I figured the two customers might be together so I telephoned the restaurant. I said, "Hey, do you see the two customers out there? Can you find out what number she's waiting for?" I watched on my iPad as the manager asked the customer for her order number. All of a sudden, her order of food appeared.

That's new-age technology working together with old-fashioned customer service.

I always checked in on the restaurants—it was part of the systems I put in place to help people stay sharp. That's why I never had an interest in franchising Portillo's or going public with it. I had the flexibility to act immediately on any kind of decision without talking to anybody or asking anybody's permission. I liked that flexibility. I could move fast, lightning-quick, and make a decision. I didn't have to ask anybody for it or wait on a vote. Sometimes I made decisions that were wrong, but fortunately most of the time they were right.

Still, the best part of my day was being in a Portillo's. I always say hello to people, both employees and customers. If there is an employee in the restaurant I had never seen or met, I find out his or her name and introduce myself. I always looked for quality in the restaurant. That's why I never played golf. I had plenty to do, and every day I wanted to make Portillo's better. I had a checklist we followed to make sure every detail was covered, from making sure that side window was washed to cleaning any dust off the ceiling fans.

I have high standards, and I looked for what the customers saw when they were in Portillo's. I walked around the entire building. Once I noticed during the lunch hour at one restaurant that an outside neon light was out. It was overcast that day and the lights were on since the restaurant opened. I informed the manager, but I was interested to also know if the closing manager the previous night had noticed it, or if anything had been done about it. Accountability helps make an operation run efficiently.

In my speech to our general managers in 2011, I stressed it was our employees who give customers "the Portillo's experience" because they've been given "the Portillo's experience." It was nearly 50 years since I opened my 6' x 12' trailer, but the values I learned over the decades still held true. I can't stress this enough.

I said, "The first step is making smart hiring decisions. I believe most every person has potential. It doesn't matter where you come from. With the right motivation and training, and a willingness to work and learn, every person can contribute. The right attitude is crucial. You can improve technical skills, but no amount of training can create drive or initiative. Our training should set them for success. Our employees should not just be another cost; they should be our most valuable asset. Employees need to see the company's interest as their own. When they do, they will voluntarily take responsibility and initiative. One way not to motivate or develop passion is to micromanage employees. Employees have to be delegated some responsibility so that they see that they have value to the overall operation.

"No single person can make an organization successful. Everyone in this room has helped make this company the successful operation it is today. Our managers are out there every day doing their part to outshine the competition. But we must never forget that the managers' success, and the company's success, depends in large part on the performance of our frontline employees. It's those employees—the patio workers, the order-takers, the cashiers—who have the most interaction with our customers and the greatest impact on our business. With smart hiring and proper direction and motivation from managers, these employees will gain that passion for what we do and will win us customers for life. That's what we need to focus on in the coming year. That's what will take us from good to great. I thank you for your hard work and dedication and am looking forward to an outstanding year."

We had an outstanding year, too. In 2012 we opened Portillo's in New Lenox, Illinois, in a shopping center with a Target and Lowe's. That set the stage for a trio of Portillo's in 2013, starting in Elgin, Illinois, and expanding into Arizona in Scottsdale and Tempe, where Chicago transplants couldn't wait for our arrival. I have always enjoyed speaking to my managers, employees, and even general audiences as a guest speaker. I love inspirational sayings, too. The staff at Portillo's probably know some of mine by heart—and may even roll their eyes when they hear them—but here a few that I am noted for, so enjoy!

"Long lines don't impress me; long lines that move fast impress me."

"My strength is that I know my weaknesses."

"A winner is someone who recognizes his God-given talents, works his tail off to develop them into skills, and uses these skills to accomplish his goals."

"Even the finest knife needs sharpening."

"If you mess up, it's not your parents' fault, so don't whine about your mistakes, learn from them."

"Your grandparents had a different word for flipping burgers—they called it 'opportunity.'"

"Your school may have done away with winners and losers, but life has not."

"What's Plan B?"

"I must constantly review myself."

"What does the customer see?"

"These rules weren't just thought up, they come from experience."

"We've got to take these people and make pros out of them."

"That's it in a nutshell."

There's not a lot of empty wall or shelf space in my homes in Oak Brook, Illinois, and Naples, Florida. I haven't been an avid collector of arts and antiques very long, but once I really focused on it in the early 2000s, I did it with the same fervor and passion I displayed daily at Portillo's. Just because I am in my seventies, this line is not synonymous with my age: I do like anything old when it comes to collecting art and antiques. It's the desire in me as a collector to possess the rare and have a piece that nobody else in the world has. The arts and antiques put my mind in a different place and time.

The start of the 21st century was a turning point for Portillo's. And for me personally, too, as I have been able to share some of my incredible journeys abroad with some amazing people. My family and friends know that I love to travel and I am a World War II buff. I made two trips to the Solomon Islands in the south Pacific within a year's span, with the first journey in late 2008. Sharon and I chartered a 165-yacht for nearly two weeks and sailed to the site of some of the bloodiest World War II battles between the U.S. and Japan. We visited the island where John F. Kennedy, the future president, swam to shore after a Japanese destroyer sank his PT boat. We also met one the locals who helped save Kennedy. We toured the remote jungle villages and discovered war relics everywhere.

Our crew of nine included retired Col. Bernard Brause, who was my former lieutenant in the Marines when I joined only a few days following my high school graduation. It was Brause who befriended me at Camp Pendleton and had such a positive influence on my life during those two years. I tracked down Brause at his home in California and asked him and his wife to make the journey with us, free of charge, to the Solomon Islands.

It was an amazing trip, the best of my life to that point. We took roughly 2,000 photographs. Nearly 1,400 U.S. Marines and more than 20,000 Japanese perished on the island of Guadalcanal. Rusted helmets, tank parts, artillery shells, and vestiges of those battles can still be found there and in the jungles. I held a luncheon on our yacht and the guest of honor was Eroni Kumana, who came aboard dressed in a bright orange T-shirt that read, I RESCUED JFK. He was probably between 85 and 90 years old. Kumana was one of the many islanders during the war who served as a scout for the Allies. He showed me on the island where he first met Kennedy. It was called Plum Pudding then but now it's called Kennedy Island. One of Kumana's sons also gave us a rusted Marine dog tag he had found years ago.

I also took Mr. William Faulkner, who was in his mid-eighties at the time, to the battlefields of Guadalcanal. Mr. Faulkner's son, David Faulkner, is a good friend. Mr. Faulkner was with the U.S. Marine Paratroopers. It was very cool to see Mr. Faulkner enjoy the trip with

David. During the first trip to the Solomon Islands, I did not go to the north end of the island. That's where, once the Japanese left the island, the Marines bivouacked, with a Japanese boat that was bombed by the Navy nearby in the water. Mr. Faulkner said it was the first time the Marines didn't have to sleep in the mud. They had hot showers and hot food. So, I took Mr. Faulkner to the north side of the island.

Mr. Faulkner remembered swimming in that area. That's where the Marines swam around and relaxed. We anchored our boat at that same exact spot offshore and I said, "Come on, Bill, let's go swimming." I pulled him around in an inner tube, and all of us there knew the history that surrounded us. Mr. Faulkner looked around and I could tell the memories came back to him. I said, "Anything look familiar Bill? Anything different?" Bill answered, "Yeah, I got swimming trunks on now."

We also visited the battlefields that Bill fought in, which included the Iron Bottom Sound Wreckage, Gavutu in Tulagi province and Vella La Vella in the Western Province, and Bloody Ridge. There's so much history there. Our guide, Bob Reynolds, a WWII veteran, had found a Japanese cannon during one of his previous trips. There was a Marine tank that had exploded and killed the three occupants. Everything there had been that way since 1942. The locals there helped us carried machetes to get through the jungles, and they never wore shoes in their life!

I have collected items from my trips to battlefields across the world. Peleliu also is the most intact WWII site in the world. There's tanks, guns, bones, and everything just lying around. There's dozens and dozens of caves that we ventured into. We saw bones, we saw ammunition. I found an old, rusted Japanese rifle. I told a military website that

"I've been to Normandy and other places like that, but the Solomon Islands was something that was completely different. It's difficult to get to. You need a boat. There's no five-star hotels, no five-star restaurants. A lot of people don't visit these outer islands. That's the beauty of a trip like this."

My life has been an amazing journey.

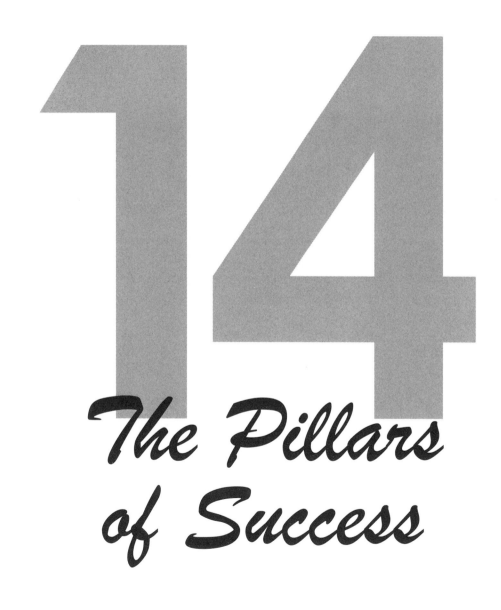

14

The Pillars of Success

My son Michael knows the business of Portillo's as well as anyone. There's not a better restaurant operations person, in my mind, in the country. Call me a little prejudiced, but I think he just plain "gets it." He started working for me as a teenager and served as vice-president of training and people development prior to the 2014 sale to Berkshire Partners. There's probably not a person who can explain the Portillo's pillars of success—quality, service, attitude, and cleanliness—better than Michael. In this piece of the book, I thought it might be most appropriate to let him share our vision in his words.

Even though Michael is a Portillo, he will be the first to say he never received any kind of special treatment from me and worked twice as hard for recognition. I even fired and rehired him once on the same night! How smart am I? He was very young and worked weekends at our Addison restaurant during the summer. Michael made 50 cents an hour and he did everything from prep the food to open and close the restaurant. He thought he had to work harder and faster, help his fellow employees, and try to provide the best guest experience for customers because he was a Portillo.

One night around the kitchen table at the house, Michael asked for a raise. He had his spiel laid out and explained what he did and how he helped at the restaurant. He didn't think I valued him enough as an employee. Michael also mentioned that his friends made $1 an hour more at their jobs, and he could probably make more if he left Portillo's. I thought about it for a moment, and he was right. I told him if he thought he could make more money working with his buddies, go for it.

I fired him.

Michael was upset and went to his bedroom. A couple of hours later, I had a change of heart because, yes, this was a family endeavor and I truly appreciated his help at the restaurant. It was true that he was a Portillo and I expected more from him than other employees. I knocked on his bedroom door and told him that he wasn't fired if he didn't want to be. Yes, I increased his pay, too. I also told him, "As you grow older, there will be people who think you are here because you are Dick Portillo's kid. I want you to earn every dollar you make so that you'll know in your heart that this is not true because that's how Dad planned it."

I've mentioned this earlier but it is worth repeating because of its importance: it was during Michael's football career in high school when I learned a valuable lesson—the hard way. I learned about the importance of family and cherishing every moment with them. I still get tears in my eyes when I think about it. I missed Michael's first touchdown reception in high school because I stayed an extra five minutes at the restaurant. I was in the school's parking lot, running to get into the game, when I heard over the stadium's loudspeakers that Michael caught a touchdown pass. And I missed it.

I couldn't tell you then—and I can't tell you today—what was so important that kept me those extra 10 minutes at the restaurant.

That's why I always stressed to my employees to embrace their families and take the time to share in those precious memories. You never get them back.

I am glad I had the smarts to rehire Michael, and I am thankful he has stuck around for all these years. It demonstrated a commitment that was such an important component of the success of Portillo's. Many folks looked for a magic wand that I waved over Portillo's. I am the first to say there was no magic wand.

It was a commitment to a series of ideas and principles that created the framework of every decision we made at Portillo's. If my team understood that and bought into those principles, making decisions became easier. I wasn't looking for my employees to follow 58,000 rules.

I wanted them to essentially follow our four pillars of success as my son Michael explains here:

QUALITY

To be as successful as my dad has been, he had to empower and engage people and create loyal followers, He created a belief system and saw no reason to over-complicate it. How he did that was by declaring our guest is the most important component in the Portillo's equation. The guest experience tops our list. What we give the customer is quality, service, attitude, and cleanliness (**Q.S.A.C.**) As simple as that sounds, we're not just talking about quality of the food. We're talking about the quality of the building, the quality of the experience, the quality of the equipment we use, the quality of the materials we use, the quality of the speakers we use, etc. Everything had to be quality, and they were specifically put in that order, too—quality, service, attitude, and cleanliness.

Our goal was to achieve the right guest experience in all those areas. If we followed through on that promise, our belief was the guest will receive and enjoy the optimal Portillo's experience and will want to return. We became a destination off of that experience. The pillars to success mandated how we made decisions. If I was managing, or I was a crew member or in any position at the restaurant, I asked myself, how does this affect the quality of visit for this guest? We empowered our employees to make a decision based on that. If they could improve the guest experience, they did.

Quality starts with your employees, the people whom we hire. People need to be proud of where they work, right? Working at Portillo's is mentally demanding. It is physically demanding. But we created an environment where they're proud to be a part of Portillo's because they knew they made a difference. Working at Portillo's is not like any other job. A lot of employees could go other places and make more money. However, many have stayed at Portillo's for years and years. Our first pillar, quality, absolutely starts with hiring the right person. We offset any challenges with our beliefs and knowing that you, as an employee, have the ability to make a difference. My dad had very high expectations and a very low tolerance—actually a zero tolerance—for a lack of quality. There was no excuse for a lack of quality in my dad's eyes. Some people may say there was a fear factor surrounding my dad. There wasn't a fear factor. The only fear factor was the fear that we all imposed on ourselves, and that was letting Mr. Portillo down. Nobody wanted to let Dad down. His commitment to us as employees and to quality created loyal followers and believers. Employees tend to work harder when there's that connection. And the thing is, it doesn't feel like work.

It is easy to say "hire quality," but the truth is finding it is difficult. I looked for personality traits that displayed a commitment or a passion or a desire to want to do the right things when I interviewed a prospective employee. If you have the personality and the drive to want to succeed, we, as managers, can help you with all the rest. We can teach employees our philosophies. We can teach employees how to do stuff they've never done before. We looked for the traits in somebody that said they cared and that wanted to try their best. As simple as that sounds, you give me somebody that says, "Hey, I am going to do the best I can and I am willing to learn," then my job is to teach and to help you be the best you can be. I believed if people knew how to be successful, they knew how to do the right thing. When I interviewed a person and that person showed me the desire to want to learn and demonstrated a commitment to try, that was usually good enough for me because we truly invested in our people.

No matter what level—be it a high school–aged crew member or a manager's position—the key is to surround yourself with quality people who have a passion and are willing to learn. We can teach them the rest, like what to put on a top bun, or how to react in certain scenarios, or how to handle cash, or how to do inventory. That's simple, basic stuff. But truly understanding how to make people engage other people, how to make them feel important and they are part of something really special, when you do that, success follows.

Quality is reflected in the products we use in Portillo's, too. There's a story that made the rounds among managers when my father was in the restaurant one day and was asked, "Why did you change your cups?" We used a very expensive cup. It wasn't made by many vendors. We could have certainly used a cheaper Styrofoam cup. We chose to use a much more expensive cup because it held the drink better. The cup didn't sweat and it wouldn't break when you carried it to your car. That's a simple example of a product that holds soda, but, again, it's a component that reflects the quality of our products.

When it came to, let's say tomatoes, quality was just as important. We used a specific size of tomatoes; one is for hot dogs and then another one is a much larger, more expensive tomato for the hamburgers. We went through great lengths to ensure that one slice of tomato covers the entire hamburger bun because we want the customer to get a piece of tomato in every bite. We didn't want to end up with two very thin slices of tomatoes; we want total coverage. We always had food vendors approach us with a cheaper product. But we asked, "What is it going to take to get these tomatoes this size and this ripeness in our door?" The produce business is really brutal. You really have to manage items like tomatoes and bananas. To be able to ensure size and ripeness, we elected to pay more and ensure the quality of the product. Vendors could always cherry-pick and say, "I can save you all this money on this product or that product." But it wasn't about the money. At Portillo's, it is about the quality of the total program. We even use a better, thicker coated wrap for our hot dogs, mainly because it is important when it comes to the quality of product.

SERVICE

If we believe that the quality experience is there, then we try to do it with the right service. And service doesn't necessarily mean being the fastest in the restaurant business. Service is a much broader term. It is about how the guests feel about their experience. We could have a long line but if that line is moving—and you've probably heard that quote before from my dad!—guests are more likely to get into it and enjoy the experience. If you create touch points with the guest by creating conversations with them or just the simple gesture of handing them a menu, accompanied with a hello and a smile, it all works.

Engagement is important. Being genuine is too. Every guest who walks into Portillo's, be it the first of the day or during the rush hour or the last customer in the door that night, we want to make contact with that person at some point. Make eye contact, say hello, do something that makes that customer feel like the most important person in the building at that time. This is where being genuine counts. You can't say, "Welcome to Portillo's, can I help you?" all day long because it no longer means anything when you routinely repeat the same generic greeting yourself. That is a waste. Make it interesting. I'd rather have an employee who changes it up and says, "Hello what can I get for you? Wow, that's really a nice shirt, where did you get it from?" I want the connection with the customer to be genuine. People say all the time, "How are you today?" But most people really don't care how you feel. They don't care what your response is. It has to be an authentic, genuine gesture and question.

When I ask a customer or an employee how they were doing, I always made a point to wait for an answer. Or I asked again. That's an important part of service. Did we engage with that person? Did we make them feel special? Erica was a longtime employee with us—her husband built my dad's second trailer and they used to live next door to us. Erica worked for us until she was 88 years old. Erica knew all the customers by name. That connection made a lasting impact. I always made a point to stop by the restaurant where she worked on her birthday. An entire section was always shut down because the tables were pulled together and filled with gifts and cakes, with a chair in the middle for Erica. All the customers came in to sing "Happy Birthday" to her. That's how she spent her birthdays, and that's how important she was to our guests.

I worked my way from the ground up and have done it all at Portillo's. I was the general manager at our restaurant in Bolingbrook (restaurant No. 5) in my mid-twenties and was promoted to general manager of Downers Grove (restaurant No. 7), which at that time was our busiest restaurant. It did crazy numbers financially and that's where Dad, who then was all about his systems and organization, put in his first drive-thru. That decision reflected his commitment to service.

Dad opened this small drive-thru as the remodeling work continued on the restaurant. It was crazy busy, and our crew was really hustling. We created what we called a "Ditto bag" system, where we literally stamped "Ditto" on a copy of the bag that went with the bag that filled the order. The drive-thru itself was an immediate success, but the process took too much time. We'd get the order in, write it on the "Ditto bag," send that to the front of the line, fill the order and get it back, and give it to the customer. It was labor intensive and really time consuming. We were really busy but we noticed we never exceeded the $470 mark in the drive-thru at our 1:00 PM reading (review sales over a certain period). No matter what we did, we couldn't break the $500 mark.

At that time customers ordered from the menu board in the drive-thru, and proceeded to the window where the order was confirmed, paid for, and picked up. Most times the drive-thru lane was so busy we could not get orders in the kitchen fast enough. I could see that Dad had something on his mind. He said, "You know the ice cream guys who come around the neighborhood at night?" I said yes, thinking he wanted to buy the staff ice cream for working so hard. He asked me, "Don't they have changers on their belts so that when you order your ice cream, they can make change for you right there?" He asked me what I thought about putting an employee outside with a walkie-talkie who communicated with an employee inside. That way we could take the customer's order and start the process. He pointed to the drive-thru line which did not appear to be moving fast enough. We couldn't take any more orders because cars could not get to the menu board fast enough. If we had an employee outside working the drive-thru, we could take the order, collect the cash, and make change.

I thought that wouldn't work, but of course, it did! By the time we had our drive-thru process running at its best, we would sometimes have eight, nine, or 10 people outside taking orders and money, often from as far away as 50 yards from the building. It was a sight to behold and today some of the biggest names in our industry are still trying to duplicate what came of that conversation I had with my dad.

ATTITUDE

Attitude is really just having the desire to please the guests. I want employees at Portillo's to come to work every day with that attitude. I know some days are more difficult than others, because we all have problems in life, right? We all come from different walks of life and have different things going on in our lives. My hope was that once an employee stepped inside Portillo's or put on his uniform, that brought a good vibe and good memories. If we have the environment that fosters the right attitude, it's likely to rub off on a guest who might be having a bad day. If the attitude of a Portillo's crew member helped make the customer feel better, that was even better. That helped create that experience we want. It's so much more than just saying, "Oh, come in to work today and have a positive attitude."

It's a choice. Attitudes are a choice, but they also are a product of your environment.

It is certainly much easier to have the right attitude if the people around you are respectful and create the right environment. It's like a chain reaction. That's why a poor attitude is something we don't tolerate. If I noticed an employee having a bad day, then it was my job to either move that employee from a contact station with guests or maybe even give them a day off. It's the environment that creates the right attitude, and it's got to be a respectful environment. My dad always said, "We are not machines. We are all going to make mistakes." Dad always trained his managers to understand that when they were dealing with a complaint, they were actually on a stage. It wasn't just the angry customer that he or she was dealing with, but the 40 or 50 others who were in line and the employees watching how they handle things.

Often, people want to prove who is right and who is wrong. Our response must be, "You know what? You are right. I missed it. I will get it for you right away." When you see the guests watching how a manager or a crew member interacts with customers, that sends a message to everyone. If a customer sees something they don't like, they are less likely to come back.

Another thing my dad always said was, "Fear is not a sustainable motivator. Respect is an invisible chain that holds people together." As a leader within the organization, you can't rule employees by fear. Dad created that level of respect, and part of the way he did it is was the way he engaged everybody, from employees to customers. That creates that invisible chain that holds people together.

I am not going to say the experience at Portillo's was great throughout for everybody. Speaking from my own personal experience, there were times I acted poorly or didn't handle an issue as well as I could have. I always tried to go back and say, "You know what? How I handled that was really poor." I made that very clear because everybody loses when it's not addressed. When you admit your mistakes, it's amazing how that respect is returned. I love that quote about the invisible chain because I hear it from my dad all the time. There's almost nothing you can't do as a team. There's nothing that you can't improve. When Dad made a decision, there's no doubt we went in that direction. But Dad probably made that decision after gathering information, hearing people out and talking to them. Sometimes it was our idea, sometimes it was his, sometimes it was a combination, and there were times we even went in a different direction once we all got together.

But when a decision was made, we went with it. We really tried to create that environment of respect from the very first day.

CLEANLINESS

When people think of an organization's pillars of success, they may not think that cleanliness should be one of them. But what better way to round off that whole experience we have been talking about, the Portillo's experience? A customer walks into the restaurant and we appeal to all of the customer's senses. You see it, you smell it, you hear it, you touch things. It starts from the moment you enter the parking lot and look at the building and hear the music. Customers should expect the quality, the service, the attitude. But something would absolutely be missing if Portillo's wasn't clean.

Our attention to detail is paramount to that success and that's why cleanliness seems like it should be a given. But all you have to do is look around the next time you are in another restaurant. It doesn't matter how good the food is. If it's not clean in the dining area, a customer may think, "I can only imagine what the kitchen looks like." Dad always was fanatical about his process and procedures. What stuck in his mind was when he took us to Disneyland as kids. He didn't see trash on the ground, anywhere. Not even a cigarette butt. Disneyland employees had those little dustpans and minibrooms and it seemed like everyone was always sweeping stuff up the second it hit the ground. Dad telephoned Portillo's from our vacation and told somebody to order the same dustpans and brooms, and he'd explain why when he returned to Chicago. Everybody should buy into the importance of cleanliness because the whole experience can be deflated by walking into a disgusting bathroom or sitting at a table that hasn't been cleaned or seeing something on the floor.

From personal experience, I never truly realized how important a clean highchair was in a restaurant until we had our first child. I go into restaurants all the time with people who have kids. I went into one with my daughter and the highchair top—you remember when they had stainless steel tops?—was disgusting. I didn't want my daughter to sit in that highchair. We implemented procedures at Portillo's to make sure our highchairs were cleaned after every use. The tray was sanitized and dried, then we put crackers and a napkin in a Portillo's hat and then covered the top with Saran Wrap so customers knew it was ready for use for their child. I didn't want any of our customers to have that same feeling I had with my child.

I have been asked which of the four pillars is the most important.

At Portillo's, we increased our sales, made our costs, and became more and more profitable for more than 50 years. Our approach was if you truly believe in the four steps of success—and it has been proven over and over again—your budget, your sales, the guest experience, that all falls in line. The hardest part is really convincing people it's that simple. When you are engaged in your brand and create an experience and trust in it, you can move mountains.

When you talk about culture, it's about the way you live. It's not about having to refer to a policy manual. It's being able to say, "I need to do this because this is how it falls into our core beliefs." The reasons the pillars go in that order— Quality, Service, Attitude, and Cleanliness—is because that is how we made our decisions. That's how we decide what's most important at that moment. If we have quality service and attitude in place, the guest is going to be more forgiving if maybe the bathroom mirror's not as clean as it should be. I'm not saying that makes it right. I'm just saying they're going to be more forgiving. But if the quality is bad, they will stop coming, I don't care how clean the place is.

It's one thing to have words on the wall or words in a manual, but if everyone involved in Portillo's doesn't truly believe how Quality, Service, Attitude, and Cleanliness affects the customer experience, then they are not going to be part of making it better. That's why our four golden rules, our pillars of success, are equally important. It's not one of four, two of four, or three of four. It's four of four. When we commit to all four pillars daily, we will optimize the Portillo's experience for our guests.

Dad's beliefs, his commitment to people, his systems, his unrelenting expectation that quality of service influences everything he does, everything he touches, has created many followers and believers. There really isn't a secret to his success. He has the uncanny ability to create an environment of respect, involvement, engagement, and empowerment that elevates people to levels even they didn't think they could reach.

His approach really applies to everything he does.

15

Gift or Curse?

There was a time in my life when I honestly thought I was the dumbest guy in the world.

I couldn't grasp things easily in school unless the subject really, really interested me. I didn't pick up things quickly. I'd review or study something two or three times and eventually I got distracted if I wasn't engaged. I couldn't focus. I'd be thinking about something and, all of a sudden, something else caught my eye.

As I have mentioned before, I was a terrible student in high school. And I think those struggles in the classroom added to my penchant for finding trouble.

Maybe it was the excitement of fighting that triggered something in my mind. I was searching for excitement. Plus, wrong as I now know it was, I believed the excitement of fighting helped take away my inferiority complex of being a slow learner. I always thought I was dumb because everybody else learned their lessons easier than I did.

If you don't pick up on things easily, you can get angry inside. And that leads you to try to take the attention off of one thing and place it on another. I was disruptive in class if the teacher looked my way and

I knew I was going to be asked to explain something. I'd rather cause a scene in class than look dumb because I didn't know the answer.

Even when I was in the Marine Corps, things were difficult for me. We had to take apart and put back together our rifle in a certain amount of time. I couldn't put it together as fast as everyone else. I looked around and was always the last one to finish. I stayed up late at night and practiced. I had to know how to take the rifle apart and put it back together again, even blindfolded at times.

I always asked myself, "Why is everybody else able to do this easier than I can?"

Though I never have been formally diagnosed with a learning disability or disorder, I have read all I can on the subjects. It was important for me to realize these challenges can affect an individual's life. I believe I have ADD, also known as ADHD. This is considered a disorder that includes difficulty staying focused and paying attention. That, in turn, made learning extremely challenging for me in school.

Despite my struggles, however, I can honestly say I was blessed with good instincts. Sharon believes I was given a gift by God. And that gift was to see things that some people don't see. And Sharon said she ultimately realized her job was to trust that gift when it came to my vision for Portillo's.

When I first heard Sharon say my gift was from God, it was a "wow" moment. I now know I am gifted in certain things and I do thank the Big Guy every morning. I haven't missed a morning of saying thanks in years. I pray to God for my kids, my wife's health, and I thank him. I thank him for that gift.

"I thank you for everything you do for me, Lord. I know it's not me; it's you. And I thank you for it."

I say this prayer every morning.

I read an article about the Nike headquarters in Beaverton, Oregon. Phil Knight had partnered with a guy named Bill Bowerman back in 1964 on a handshake and they each contributed $500 a piece to start the company. This article featured one of the displays which had a tennis shoe stuck in a waffle iron.

In the early years of the company, Bowerman was inspired by a waffle iron to develop a sole that was lighter and provided more traction for runners. Who could have imagined that a waffle iron inspired a running shoe that would become the basis for an iconic international brand? (In November 2015, *Forbes* magazine named Knight the 15th-richest person in the world, with an estimated net worth of $28.1 billion).

How's that for thinking out of the box? I've always thought out of the box, too.

I never wanted to be like everybody else and that's why the Portillo's brand is so unusual. Once you have confidence in your instincts, you must never be dissuaded by other people's refusal to believe or to refute what you instinctively know is true. Your instincts draw the blueprint for success. Don't give up on your instincts just because they don't seem to fit into a formula. A lot of people avoid going into business because they're afraid. There's the fear factor of the unknown.

I'll tell you without blinking an eye that fear teaches you to be cautious and careful. It also forces the individual to be creative and compassionate, because some people just drop the ball and stick their heads in the sand and don't go any further at times. Often fear becomes the fuel for your power. Fear was my fuel. I was scared when

I opened my hot dog stand in that shopping lot parking lot more than 50 years ago. It forced me to become creative and think out of the box.

And people to this day ask me, "Why a hot dog stand?"

In the years before I opened that stand, I kicked around doing all kinds of crazy jobs. I mean, think about it: unloading box cars, driving a truck, working construction, working at Inland Steel, working in a forging plant, all that. I couldn't do those jobs forever. I was tired. I was strong and young but I thought, "What's going to happen down the line? How long can I do this?" And then I saw some of those guys in those factories who were older than I was, and it just looked to me like they were working without a future. That's not where I wanted to be. So how would I get out of there?

I wish I could claim genius, but it was simple: I always loved hot dogs. And I loved the smell of the hot dog cart when you walked up to it. There was something about, it had a…I don't know if mystique is the right word, but it had an aura about it. It had the smell. It had a culture. It was hard to explain but I knew I loved it. The guy with the steamer—he would open it up and the steam would hit him right in his face. And he'd slap mustard on the hot dog. It was just the moves, the excitement of it. I don't know. That's the best way I can explain it. Honestly, I don't know how better to put it.

My instincts told me that I had to make sure nobody had the jump on us, not even if it was the little hot dog stand down the street after we had become successful. Why? Because I was that little guy once. Those are the guys I fear the most. I was once that guy and I never forget that some people dismissed what I might ultimately be capable of. The guys you think are small or insignificant, they could come up and eat you alive.

Nobody holds the record forever. That's why we celebrated plateaus at Portillo's. We celebrated achievements that nobody else had done, but we also wanted to make sure we got better—always. What can we do next? There were many times when I knew we had a good thing going. I knew we were good and profitable as a business. Our sales were up, the competition wasn't even close to us. But I always said, "Mark my words. The competition will close the gap." They will spend more money on décor, they will spend more money on labor, they will upgrade their food offerings, and they will narrow the gap. That's why I always asked, "What's next?" I had to rely on my instincts. As soon as you think you are at the top of the mountain, there's only one way to go.

And that's down. "Don't get comfortable" was always my motto. I always tried to tell that to my supervisors and staff. We are on top of the game, we are on top of the mountain. But don't get cocky and don't get comfortable.

I honestly believe a lot of people have those instincts but don't follow up on them. They don't understand what's happening. I have a learning disability but so did people like Steve Jobs, Richard Branson, Charles Schwab, and Henry Ford. But if you look at all those people, they did something that was out of the box. They did something different than anyone else was doing. People are afraid of leaving their comfort zone. I believe that. At one time or another, we are all in a comfort zone. People love it. It's a natural feeling. And people are afraid to take chances and follow their instincts. And that's what those guys did.

That's what I did.

Here are a few highly successful and driven people who have been diagnosed with learning disabilities:

Olympian Michael Phelps: He was formally diagnosed with ADHD when he was in fifth grade. After being on Ritalin for over two years, Phelps chose to stop using the drug and instead used swimming to help him find focus. He ended his Olympic career as the most highly decorated Olympian of all time, boasting 22 medals (18 gold).

Film director Steven Spielberg: Spielberg was diagnosed with dyslexia at age 60. He learned to read two years after his classmates and said he was bullied so much that he dreaded going to school. He offers this advice to students and young adults with learning disabilities: "You are not alone, and while you will have dyslexia for the rest of your life, you can dart between the raindrops to get where you want to go. It will not hold you back."

Businessman/investor Charles Schwab: Schwab bluffed his way through his early years of schooling by reading comic book versions of books like *Ivanhoe* and *A Tale of Two Cities*. While attending Stanford University, Schwab was initially floundering, failing both freshman English and French." With a net worth of more than $5.1 billion, Schwab still finds reading and writing tedious.

Entrepreneur Richard Branson: Branson is proclaimed to be "the only person in the world to have built eight billion-dollar companies from scratch in eight different countries." Unlike many who consider dyslexia a curse, Branson calls it his "greatest strength." Growing up in a time when dyslexia was largely mis-understood, Branson's teachers simply labeled him as lazy or "not very clever." After starting up a successful alternative news-paper in high school, he was confronted by his headmaster who said, "Congratulations, Branson. I predict that you will either go to prison or become a millionaire."

Entrepreneur Steve Jobs: Jobs, who passed away in October 2011, was the chairman, chief executive officer (CEO), and a co-founder of Apple Inc; CEO and majority shareholder of Pixar; a member of The Walt Disney Company's board of direc-tors following its acquisition of Pixar; and founder, chairman, and CEO of NeXT.

Businessman Paul Orfalea: Orfalea struggled in school due to ADHD and dyslexia, which even lead to his expulsion from four of the eight schools he attended. In the end, Orfalea grad-uated high school with a 1.2 GPA and went on to attend the University of Southern California. While still only getting C's and D's in college, he was working part time on a business venture he called Kinko's. In an interview, he attributed his success in part to his conditions: "My learning disability gave me certain advantages, because I was able to live in the moment and capitalize on the opportunities I spotted."

Each night before I go to bed, I scribble notes to myself on a small sheet of paper or sticky note and put it on the bedstand. It's my to-do list for the next day. There might be three things, four things, 10 things I want to get done the following day. And I love to cross them off. "Got to that one. What's next? Let's go." I may sit up in bed in the middle of the night and write something down. That's not always efficient. There are times when I get up in the morning and I can't read my own writing!

I am an early riser, too. I get up at 5:00 every morning. I may think of something or have an idea, so I will telephone Patty Sullivan, my assistant, and leave a voicemail on her office phone. When Patty arrives in the office and checks her voicemail, she may have numerous messages from me, and we will discuss them when I get into the office.

I love to stay busy and I attack my daily lists aggressively. Maybe I learned it in the Marines.

In the summer of 2017, for example, my to-do list one day featured an afternoon business meeting. I met with a young couple about their ice cream business. I had to convince them to change—without ruining their dreams or them thinking they weren't qualified because they had so much passion. And I loved that passion. But there wasn't anything unique about their ice cream shop. It was the same as thousands of other ice cream shops across the country. I had to convince them the importance of making their business more unique than anyone else's. I had to convince them this was the right move for them as a young, aggressive couple. I am the landlord of the building and I will finance the business. But I had to convince them and show them the way that I operated. This is the culture I created. I needed to know if they agreed with me or not and convince them this was the right decision and in their best interests. I had to look at their faces. I had to look at their expressions. I had to see it in their eyes.

That was on my list that day. I scribbled a reminder to myself: "Convince them, but don't scare them."

My instincts fuel my competitiveness. And that showed up on my to-do notes, too.

I told Patty one morning I wanted to talk to one of the guys I was involved with on a boutique hotel project in Tempe, Arizona. Across from our project, there was an open lot where an investor was trying to attract another group to help him build a hotel. I thought, "Competition right across the street. My god. I don't like that." But this gentleman was having trouble getting the finances, and that was why he was trying to get another investor involved.

I telephoned one of the guys I am partners with and told him, "Here's what I want to do. I want to purchase an ad in the local newspaper and place signs around our project site." I wanted to let the community—and the competition—know this hotel group, noted for the most unique boutique hotels in the country, is going to build on this spot. And behind the group is Dick Portillo, the wealthy businessman, blah, blah blah, who already has financed the project. So, we did that. And our competitor couldn't get any other investors involved.

That's business. I didn't take anything away from my competitor's wife or children or anything like that. I soon added another note to my to-do list on that same project, reminding my partner, "That was shot one. Let's keep the pressure on and keep the marketing on there so nobody touches that land."

I was at a function and a couple of physicians asked me, "What school did you go to? What business college did you go to?" They were customers of mine and both are surgeons. I told them I was a terrible student in high school, because I have this learning disability and nothing ever worked the right way for me. I always thought differently. So, I have followed my instincts. They asked again, "What's your educational background?"

I said, "Asphalt University."

They had a confused look on their faces. I was educated on the streets because I followed my instincts all the way down the line. Most of the time those instincts proved to be correct. That was my college education. I didn't try to be like McDonald's or anyone else. I said my approach is working and God blessed me. I might not be the greatest mind in certain things, like academics. But I believe my learning disability has helped me do other things in my life in terms of thinking outside of the box. I think in certain ways it is an advantage—and not a disadvantage—to have a learning disability. Who decided to use the term "learning disability"? It's just as easy to put it under "learning enhancement" in my case.

I was the guest speaker at Elmhurst College in Elmhurst, Illinois. There had to be more than 800 people there, a full house. And I mentioned I had a learning disability and it always bugged me. I explained I thought my mind worked in different ways and I believed my learning disability was an advantage, not a disadvantage. I didn't think like everyone else and that helped me be successful. You could hear a pin drop when I spoke.

What brand in the country today is more unique than Portillo's? When we opened a Portillo's in Woodbury, Minnesota, we made $351,000 after sales tax during the first week. But that's not our record.

That happened in Scottsdale, Arizona, in 2013. We made $438,000 in the first six days. Nobody has done that in the country. Think about it. Not Steak 'n Shake. Not McDonald's. Not Burger King. Nobody in the country has ever done it. We are a small company but we had 33 million transactions in 2016. How does that happen? Why in this field—the restaurant business is the most competitive business in the country—does that happen? Nobody can argue with that. But how does that happen? Why is it then that Portillo's can not only compete with the big guns but beat the hell out of them?

The answer is its uniqueness and its experience.

And that uniqueness is my willingness not to think like others. Folks may think if you have ADHD, you are all over the place. I was distracted when something didn't interest me. But when I am intensely interested in a subject, I am the most attentive, directed individual there is. That's how I got interested in Colorado mining. I picked up every book I could on ghost towns and every book I could on gold and silver and lead and the mountains of Colorado. I mean, I read everything I could get my hands on about Colorado mining. I rented a four-wheeler and even went to the old mining towns. I took photographs. I collected mining artifacts and put them in my 16th restaurant in Naperville, Illinois. I put a lot of love in that restaurant. I have a wagon and a neon horse with its legs moving suspended from the ceiling, and customers walk down a mine shaft to the bathrooms. It was a lot of fun to design the interior of that restaurant.

And being a former Marine, I read all these Marine books, too, like *Helmet for My Pillow*, *Old Breed*, *Killing the Rising Sun*, and *Guadalcanal Diary*. I just read one right after another, after another, after another. Then I thought, "I want to go to the places that I have read about." I made four trips to the Solomon Islands and other trips to Bougainville, New Guinea; Saipan, Peleliu; and Iwo Jima, where Marines fought some vicious battles. When I get really interested in something, I focus on it. And then my memory seems to be okay.

I know I think differently. But I also know I don't want to fail. I want to be the best. I also understand it's great to be at the top but it's really hard to stay there. I have a people who watch me to see what I am going to do next. I didn't have time to dwell after Portillo's sold. I was like, "What's next? What do I want to get invested in? What can I do more? And better?" That drives me to this day. It might be the fear of being stagnant or I realize my own mortality. I need a project. I am constantly in motion. I have always been preparing to open the next restaurant, been thinking about the next item for the menu, and planning the next trip. I have never picked up a golf club. I don't take naps. How do people take a "snooze" during the day? I can't sit around all day, read a book, eat dinner, and go to bed. I have to be moving. I like being in control.

I used to say, "You can't control the weather—yet."

As Portillo's became more and more successful, that gave me confidence. It was my whole life because I was comfortable with it. I knew I was making the right decisions. I was in charge, I knew what I was doing, and I was doing something that nobody else had done. The formula was working. That's probably why my life revolved around Portillo's—I was comfortable with it. I didn't read anything out of a book that said, "Hang in there." It just worked. I was really comfortable in my surroundings.

I am grateful for those instincts and, as I said. I thank the Big Guy every day.

I consider that a wonderful gift. Not a curse.

16

Only in America

In a hallway outside my Oakbrook Terrace office is a sculpture titled "Self-Made Man." The 37-inch bronze piece, by Bobbie Carlyle of Loveland, Colorado, depicts a man carving himself out of stone, carving his character, carving his future. The sculpture was a Christmas gift from my lovely wife of 59 years in 2016.

When Sharon gave the statue to me, she said if there was ever a self-made man who was able to live the American Dream, it was me.

Who would believe my journey? The son of immigrants from Mexico and Greece who spent time in the projects of Chicago, struggled in school due to a learning disability, joined the Marines straight out of high school, toiled in what seemed like every grimy factory in Chicago, married and went to work on the same day, took our $1,100 life savings and opened a hot dog stand in Villa Park in 1963, and 51 years later built it into a restaurant empire?

I wouldn't believe it myself if I hadn't lived it. I hit the jackpot, and every morning I thank the Big Guy upstairs. I know there are people who might look at my journey and say, "What's so complicated about what the guy did? It's a hot dog stand." I am here to say it's not a hot dog stand. It's an experience. How do I convince the public that Portillo's is extremely complex? I know people have said, "What is the big deal? The guy's selling hot dogs. There's hot dog places all over the place."

True. But how many of them reached the pinnacle Portillo's has?

I have traveled the world. I have been nearly everywhere in the Caribbean. I have been to islands in the Pacific, where the people don't wear shoes and have never worn shoes. I have been in so many different countries around the globe where they don't have any opportunities at all. We have so many opportunities in the United States. It is here that a guy like me, not too smart of a guy academically, can reach the heights that I've reached. How many countries could you do that in? Not too many. This is still truly the land of opportunity.

I know there's a lot of technology "startups" in the world today, but I will say this and I honestly believe it: the easiest way for the average person to make it today is in the food industry, because how many people are that tech savvy? I still see people who have a great idea. The hot dog stand my wife and I used to go to and where I got my inspiration is still in business. They have been serving hot dogs for more than 60 years. They could have done so many more things with their business because it is a great product. But they're in the hot dog business, that's all. They have hot dogs and soda. That is their comfort zone. They didn't want to go through possibly the sacrifices and the aggravation and the rejections and everything you have to do to reach the next level.

I have the imagination. I have the passion. I was never comfortable. I always wanted more and I always had that fear of being poor. I didn't want to be poor ever again. But if you put all that aside, and you really have a passion for what you want to do and the confidence to try what others won't, you can do pretty much anything you want in this country and be successful.

Here are a few unique entrepreneurs and how they have made it in the food business by thinking outside the box.

Tim McEnery

Tim started Cooper's Hawk Winery & Restaurants at the age of 29 in 2005 in Orland Park, Illinois. Tim has grown it into a competitive retail operation generating nearly $300 million in annual revenue with 35 restaurants and an award-winning winery. The Cooper's Hawk wine collection has garnered more than 400 awards while McEnery has received multiple accolades including *Crain's Chicago Business'* "40 Under 40", Ernst & Young's "2014 Midwest Entrepreneur of the Year," and the LEAD Award from HR.com. The concept is a fusion of familiar elements—winery, modern casual restaurant, Napa-style tasting room, and artisanal retail market—that has combined to create an entirely new hospitality experience, according to the company's website. Tim and his family have been on my boat in Naples, Florida, several times.

Jimmy John Liautaud

Jimmy founded Jimmy John's, a franchised sandwich restaurant chain that specializes in delivery, in 1983, in Charleston, Illinois (his first store was in a garage). In 30 years, the company has grown to more than 2,500 locations in nearly all 50 states. Jimmy also has traveled a nontraditional journey into the upper level of business. And, in his own words, here's how he accomplished it:

I think that I was always a survivor, and I always had a couple of bucks in my pocket. So, I didn't know any other way. I mean,

I didn't have the option. And sometimes not having a plan B is kind of a good thing. Not being able to live in your parents' house, and not being able to have guaranteed government assistance, and not having, sort of, a guaranteed stack of firewood, somehow, kind of forces people to really become who they are. And it certainly did me. I never had the option, and never had a plan B. And so, I made hay.

In the restaurant business, we are paid for our own discomfort. We're not paid for a genius idea. You know, it's not genius to make a great cheeseburger. You can do that pretty good, but to do it 24/7/365, any way your customer wants it, whenever they want it, however they want it, with a smile on your face, and whether it's snow, wind, or rain, or the power goes out, or whatever, your customers expect that product from you. And if you're willing to sacrifice, and you're willing to put yourself in those uncomfortable situations, late nights, weekends, no weddings, no funerals, and you sacrifice all that, in this industry you can kick ass and you will succeed way more than anybody else.

If you're willing to make that sacrifice—Dick did it and I did it—you can be incredibly successful in our industry, but you've got to be willing to do it. There's no silver bullets. You know, at Jimmy John's we don't have meetings, because people do what we do, not what we say. So, we just go in there and just lead by example, and then they follow, or they don't.

I am not sure if anyone really knows where the first hot dog on a bun was served in the United States. Pick your favorite story and stick to it.

According to the 2008 book *Never Put Ketchup on a Hot Dog* by Bob Schwartz—the book is on Chicago's hot dog passion—Schwartz writes it has been suggested that the "hot dog on a bun was first introduced during the Louisiana Purchase Exposition in St. Louis in 1904 by a Bavarian concessionaire who loaned white gloves to his patrons for them to hold hot sausages."

The story goes on to say that "since many of the gloves were not returned, he needed to come up with a better idea. So, he asked his brother-in-law, a baker, for help. The baker improvised and made some long soft rolls to fit the sausages—thus the introduction of the hot dog bun."

Of course, baseball and hot dogs go together like balls and strikes.

Sausage was a standard fare at baseball parks near the turn of the 19th century. The tradition is believed to have been started by St. Louis bar owner Chris Von de Ahe, a German. There's also the legend of Babe Ruth, the New York Yankees slugger and "Sultan of Swat" from 1914 to 1935, who, it was said, routinely ate anywhere from 12 to 24 hot dogs between doubleheaders. According to the National Hot Dog and Sausage Council's survey of hot dog and sausage consumption at major league ballparks in the United States, ballparks sold 19.4 million hot dogs in 2016. While the Chicago Cubs won the 2016 World Series, Los Angeles Dodgers fans consumed a MLB-high 2.6 million hot dogs that season. According to the Nielsen Company, Chicago ranked sixth in the top hot dog consuming cities in 2016 behind Los Angeles, New York, Philadelphia, Boston, and Phoenix;

and Chicago was second in top sausage consuming cities behind Los Angeles.

These millions and millions of sales leads to another question. Where did the creation of the term "hot dog" come from?

Some say, according to Schwartz's book, that "hot dog" was coined in 1901 at the Polo Grounds in New York on a "cold day early in the baseball season. Vendors were hawking their dachshund sausages by saying they were 'red hot.'" Tad Dorgan, a New York sports cartoonist, "had observed the scene and drew a cartoon of a barking dachshund sausage nestled in a roll. Since he did not know how to spell "dachshund," he simply wrote "hot dog."

I know the feeling Dorgan must have had when he realized he couldn't spell "dachshund"—if the story is true, because nobody has ever found a copy of that cartoon—because I didn't know how to cook a hot dog when I opened my hot dog stand in 1963! And that is a true story. This is true, too. I love hot dogs and their place in Chicago's history.

A hot dog, also known as a frankfurter, is a cooked sausage. The word "frankfurter" comes from Frankfurt, Germany, where pork sausages similar to hot dogs originated. It has been said the popular sausage also was called a "little-dog" sausage and was created in the late 1600s by Johann Georghehner, a butcher living in Coburg, Germany. It has been said, according to stories, that Georghehner traveled to Frankfurt to promote his new product.

German immigrants were part of the United States since the revolution, but it wasn't until the mid-1800s when they started to heavily populate the Midwest. The Germans dominated Chicago's meat industry. In 1880, it is estimated that 36 percent of all butchers in the city were German immigrants and many more were German origin, according to a story written by Matthew Spina on Thrillist.com titled "A History of the Esteemed Chicago-style Hot Dog" published in 2016.

The story continued, "The frankfurters they brought with them were the perfect industrial food item. Chicago was the meatpacking capital of the world, butchering hogs and cattle from all over the Midwest, and thus was a leader in the industrialization of food. The introduction of steam-powered meat choppers allowed Chicago factories to turn less desirable meat trimmings, from their plants in the Union Stock Yards, into the affordable street food. Chicago's oldest hot dog brand, David Berg, was founded in 1860, and national brands like Armour and Oscar Mayer soon followed."

Schwartz writes in his book that two "Austro-Hungarian immigrants brought their old-world sausage recipes to the Columbian Exposition World's Fair of 1893 in Chicago. Samuel Ladany and Emil Reicht sold their sausages to enthusiastic throngs of people at the fair and a year later opened their first company store at 1215 South Halsted Street." I was there many times years ago (it's no longer there).

Spina's story added about Ladany and Reicht, "They made a big splash with their popular stand selling dogs on the street at the Columbian Exposition. They made so much money they used the proceeds to invest in a larger business and named it after the pinnacle of sausage cities, Vienna Beef. To this day Vienna uses the original natural-casing, all-beef recipe developed by Jewish immigrants that gives the Chicago dog its distinctive flavor profile, snap, and texture." I am good friends with the Vienna Beef people today. Jim Bodman, chairman and CEO of Vienna Beef, and I are good friends. He's quite the character and we have had a lot of laughs. He's a great businessman and he has done a tremendous job with Vienna.

If Jim telephoned me right now and asked me for a million dollars, I'd answer, "You want a check or you want that in cash?" I wouldn't hesitate because he's that good of a friend. One of the nicest gifts I have received was from Jim, who is a talented craftsman and woodworker. There was a tree near our first trailer in Villa Park and Jim chopped off a dead limb and made a pen and pencil set from it for me. I couldn't believe it. Talk about a gift from the heart. I was so appreciative of that gift you would have thought Jim had given me $100 million.

Others point to college magazines where the word "hot dog" began appearing in the 1890s. It says at Yale in the fall of 1894, "dog wagons" sold hot dogs at the dormitories. As far as Chicago's love for the hot dog, Spina wrote, "By the 1920s Maxwell St. on the West Side was the center of Chicago's immigrant community. A bustling market where Jewish, Italian, Greek, and Polish traders would sell clothes, trinkets, and food. Hot dogs were the dominant meal for the busy cost-conscious crowds that would fill the streets hawking their wares.

"Many of these vendors also owned vegetable stands, and they began to experiment with a wide range of toppings plucked fresh from the market. After the market crash in 1929, hot dogs went from a favorite cheap-eat to a necessity. Just as selling them has sustained generations of immigrants, eating hot dogs sustained out-of-work Americans. While other industries crumbled, hot dog vendors became even bigger community mainstays."

Fluky's opened in Chicago in 1929 on Maxwell and Halsted streets and was founded by Abe Drexler. It's self-acknowledged as the originator of the Chicago-style hot dog. The store's "Depression Sandwich" was a frankfurter on a bun with mustard, pickle, relish, onion, dill pickle, hot peppers, lettuce, and tomatoes, accompanied by French fries, for 5 cents. Fluky's—still owned by the Drexler family—maintains a stand in Niles, Illinois. As soldiers returned home from World War II, Spina wrote "they looked to a better life just like their immigrant fathers. Now second or third generation, they would carry the Chicago dog out from western Chicago to the rest of the city."

So, there you have it, even if it's the abbreviated version. While the hot dog's precise history may never be known, this much is known: it continues to be one of America's favorite foods. Check out these 2016 statistics from The National Hot Dog and Sausage Council:

On Independence Day, Americans will enjoy 150 million hot dogs, enough to stretch from D.C. to L.A. more than five times

Los Angeles residents consume more hot dogs than any other city (more than 36 million pounds), beating out New York and Philadelphia.

Chicago's O'Hare International Airport consumes six times more hot dogs—725,000 more—than Los Angeles International Airport and LaGuardia Airport combined.

During peak hot dog season, from Memorial Day to Labor Day, Americans typically consume 7 billion hot dogs. That's 818 hot dogs consumed every second during that period.

Years ago, a math teacher who was a customer in my Bolingbrook, Illinois, restaurant told me there were 256 ways to dress a hot dog. It's like the telephone. There's only 10 numbers, but look at how many combinations you get. Truthfully, a true Chicago hot dog hasn't changed over the decades. The dog is dressed in mustard, onion, relish, tomato, pickle, and peppers—sorry, no ketchup.

You never want to put ketchup on a hot dog. It's a Chicago thing, though there are others across the country who agree. According to my oldest son Michael, the reasoning is ketchup was designed to cover up bad meat. The National Hot Dog & Sausage Council, the official trade association in Washington, D.C., has the rule in its paper on "Hot Dog Etiquette and everyday guidance for eating America's sacred food." It says, "Don't use ketchup on your hot dog after the age of 18." (Children love the sweetness of ketchup, so they get a pass and are allowed to spread ketchup on their hot dogs).

I never wanted to put ketchup on a hot dog. If a customer asked for ketchup, I'd say, "I don't like to put ketchup on the hot dog," in a joking manner. But the customer always wins, so I'd do it.

When I opened The Dog House in 1963, I quickly discovered it was hard to put a food cost on a hot dog. I could if it was just a hot dog in a bun, or maybe just a hot dog, a bun, and mustard. I figured out how many scoops I got out of a gallon of mustard. But there are hundreds of ways to make a hot dog: mustard, relish, onion, tomato, pickle, pepper, or any combination of those. I first sold hot dogs with mustard, relish, onion, and peppers. Later on, I added a tomato and pickle. At one time, I also put cucumber on it. So, there's six items on there, not including the cucumber. Depending on what the customer wanted, I served the hot dog naked (no dressings), a combination of the items, or all of them. There's a lot of combinations. So how do you put a food cost on it?

There's nothing more symbolic of Chicago than its hot dog. And as people came in from Chicago and moved to the suburbs, they wanted hot dogs. They loved them. I sold thousands and thousands from my first trailer. And I had to be really fast when I made them. Really, really fast, because I only had two steamers at the time. And there was a smell. I opened the windows in the summertime and the people would come up and say, "Oh boy, it smells good. Smells good." That always stuck in my mind and it remained part of a complex formula that made Portillo's an exciting destination.

It has been an unbelievable ride. People still ask me, "Why didn't you franchise Portillo's?" I could have sold thousands of franchises over the years. I received calls all the time. Franchise, franchise, franchise. But I believed it would dilute the idea that I set up. When you franchise, you don't own it. People love you and they buy the franchise. But then they're going to try to change things. They don't love you anymore. Once they get the franchise and they realize that you don't own it, they try to change it. It never crossed my mind to franchise. Never for a moment.

That would have ruined my American dream.

All the experiences—good, bad, and unexpected—over the years are an important part of my journey.

It was in the late 1970s when Sharon and I were living in Addison, west of Chicago. We had a tremendous snowstorm and people were stranded in their cars on the tollway near our home. Sharon and I had built a fire in the fireplace and opened a bottle of champagne. The snow was really falling, perfect for a fire and a quiet night. I could see the tollway from our house and I noticed the flicker of headlights. Cars were stopped in their tracks in the snow.

I told Sharon I had to see what was happening. I borrowed my neighbor's snowmobile and headed toward the tollway a quarter mile away. When I got there my first thought was, "Oh, this is a crisis. Holy cow." A woman and her teenage son were in the first car I approached. I asked her if they were okay. I told her, "I know I look suspicious and all that, but I live right down the street and we have a warm fire." She answered, "Well, I am almost out of gas." I told her to turn off the car and I'd give them a ride to my house. She trusted me, and we all walked into the living room. Sharon was by the fireplace, drinking a glass of champagne. I said, "Sharon, there are problems on the tollway and these people need some help."

I said earlier that Sharon is the kindest person I know, and she proved it again—even though, initially a bit surprised, she may have said, "Who in the heck are these people?" I jumped on the snowmobile and headed back to the tollway. We ended up with around 20 people in our home that evening. There was nowhere for them to go. We thought one woman had a baby wrapped in a blanket, but it was her dog. The only thing these people had in common was they were stranded. We were low on food because Sharon had planned to go grocery shopping the following day, but she cooked whatever we had in the cabinets and we tried to feed everyone. It was a slumber party. We actually had a pleasant evening getting to meet and talk to these strangers. They were scattered all over the house. Everyone spent the night and left the next morning. The local newspaper found out about what we did and wrote a short story on it.

I also have had so many wonderful employees over the years. They played such an important role in the success of Portillo's. Without them, I would not have been able to accomplish what we did. Glenda Knippen worked for me nearly 50 years, starting in high school while we were in the second trailer and working her way up to be benefits manager of Portillo's. So many employees have started at a young age and have had successful careers. It was and still is a family affair.

Glenda worked for Sears during high school but I hired her after she graduated and needed a job. Her future husband, Dan, also worked for me prior to that for a short period of time when I first opened in 1963. Dan was a freshman in high school. Sadly, I found out Dan's father didn't treat him well. It wasn't a good situation. Making matters worse, his father cashed Dan's paychecks and didn't leave his son any money. I gave Dan two paychecks—one to give to his father and one for him to keep. I am not even sure his father ever realized it. When Dan's father died a short time later, the teenager didn't have anywhere to go. Sharon and I decided to take him into our family and we raised him like our son. Dan graduated from high school and was drafted, serving in the Vietnam War. When Dan returned, I asked him to manage our hot dog stand in Glendale Heights.

Dan was a few years older than Glenda and they met in the second trailer. Glenda lived within walking distance of our expanded hot dog stand in the parking lot of the Village DuPage Shopping Center. Her first day on the job I gave her a 90-minute crash course on how to prepare a hot dog, how to cook the fries, how run the cash register (the one with the big keys that you had to really mash down), the whole nine yards. Glenda was a quick learner, too. I had to run an errand and told her, "You're going to be fine." And she was. Glenda and Dan were married when he returned from Vietnam and Dan worked for us for almost 50 years. Unfortunately, Dan is no longer with us; he passed away in June of 2012. Glenda is one of the few employees who saw where we started and was part of where we ended. It has been such a fantastic experience.

Maybe it was a combination of luck and timing. I know I wanted to prove to people I wasn't a screw-up because I wasn't the smartest kid, far from it. I had no idea when I opened my first hot dog stand I'd become what I am today. I had a series of dead-end jobs and knew I had to make a move before it was too late. I wanted to build something, be in charge, and make a few bucks. There was that constant need to prove myself. At first, the hot dog stand was another job. I didn't know what I was doing and had a limited menu. I sneaked into a rival business to learn where he purchased his hot dogs, buns, and condiments. The first few years were difficult but I stuck with it, and the customers liked my hot dogs. That made me feel so good. It was like my drug of choice. As the lines grew, so did my confidence. I never stopped working, pushing toward a milestone in every hour of my life. Every hour, every day, every week, every month, every year, I wanted to be better. I prompted a new phrase in restaurant lexicon in "fast-casual dining" and hoped to make a customer's visit to Portillo's an experience.

In Bob Schwartz's book *Never Put Ketchup on a Hot Dog*, he wrote this about me:

> There have been some great hot dog stand operators over the years. But no one has come anywhere close to the kind of

success of one particular man who is now considered to be the hot dog king of Chicago. I'm referring to Dick Portillo. From Near West suburban, humble beginnings in Villa Park to his "mega-stands" of today, Portillo's has actually created a totally unique niche restaurant that combines old hot dog stand sandwiches and quality with spacious surroundings, a variety of menu choices, and an entertaining nostalgic backdrop of past eras in Chicago. From those flapper days of the 1920s to the doo-wop days of the 1950s, Dick has transformed his restaurants and our imagination to a food trip down memory lane.

I understand my wealth has afforded me and my family some wonderful luxuries and a wonderful life. I love being out on the water on my 130-foot Westport and I really love to fish and take long excursions tracing historical routes, including those of Christopher Columbus. I have taken my boat through the Panama Canal, all over the Bahamas, Alaska, the Caribbean, and Mexico.

What helps put my own personal journey into perspective are two large photos, only a few feet apart from each other, in the hallway of my Oakbrook Terrace office. One is of the Mother Francis Cabrini housing projects on Mohawk Street where I spent part of my childhood. The other is an aerial view of my home in Oak Brook, Illinois. The few feet between those photos remind me every day how far I have come as a "Self-Made Man."

I am a living proof that the American dream can be achieved.

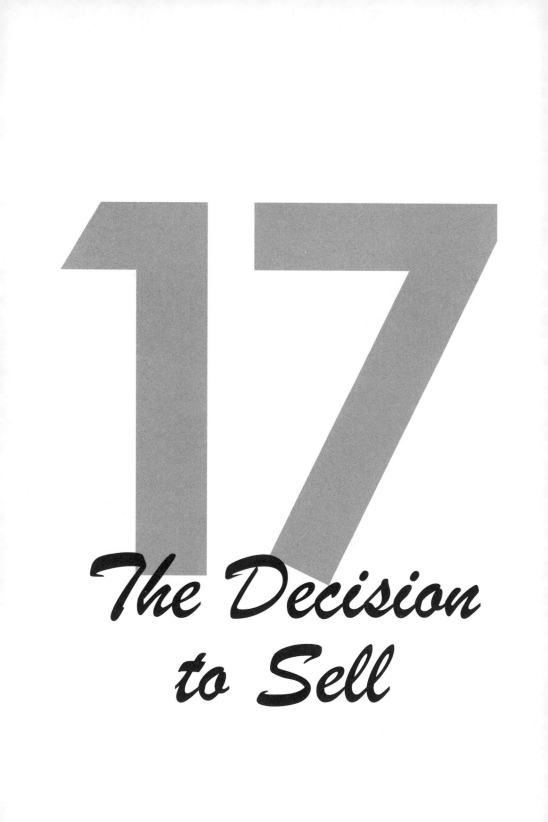

17

The Decision to Sell

I thought Damon Chandik was stalking me.

I say that jokingly, but it seemed every time I was at a Portillo's, or we had a grand opening at a new store in 2012 and 2013, I saw Damon in the crowd. I kid you not. I may have been in California, Chicago, or Arizona, and, guess what? There was Damon, a good-looking guy who was dressed as if he stepped right off of fraternity row. I laughed and said to him, "Oh, you were just in the neighborhood?"

Actually, the neighborhood was changing. And Damon caught me at the right time.

Damon Chandik is the managing director and co-head of consumer investment banking/head of restaurant investment banking for Piper Jaffray Companies. PJC is a full-service investment bank and asset management firm focused on mergers and acquisitions. Damon is based in California and focuses on restaurants. He was once named one of the top 50 most influential people in the restaurant industry by *Nation's Restaurant News*.

Damon is a huge fan of Portillo's. He first visited our restaurants more than 20 years ago when he was on business, stopping in for an Italian beef or Italian sausage sandwich. Even from the outside looking in, Damon felt Portillo's was a phenomenal company just by talking to our customers. He said he always wanted to be involved in Portillo's and help in any way he could if he ever had an opportunity.

Damon had tried to get in contact with me numerous times but he hadn't had much luck. He finally connected with Karen Peterson, our CFO and longtime employee, at our corporate office in Oak Brook, Illinois, outside of Chicago. That's how the introductions and our conversations initially started. And, two years later in August of 2014, with Damon's persistence and help, I sold 38 Portillo's, nine Barnelli's, and two commissary locations across Illinois, Indiana, California, and Arizona to the private-equity firm Berkshire Partners out of Boston.

I say that with a skip in my heart because it's still an emotional moment for me. Not because of the money involved, but because of what I had accomplished over 50-plus years in the business. I think it's those strong memories and my passion for the business that occasionally cause me to have some regrets over selling Portillo's. But I think that's normal, and those emotions pass when I think about how blessed I have been.

I am immensely proud of Portillo's. It was a brand and culture that defied the odds and generated per-store revenue that is unheard of in fast food or fast-casual restaurants.

An average McDonald's in the United States, for example, brings in nearly $2.5 million in annual revenue, with breakfast making up 28 to 30 percent of that. The average newer Portillo's brings in more than $8 million. And hot dogs are only 12 percent of our sales. Our higher-volume locations can sell around $2 million of salads a year alone. Salads! Why would I sell? I had all the money I wanted and was making $60 million annually. I didn't have any debt—other than Sharon's Neiman Marcus credit card! My employees were happy, too. But I also realized the next step—to plow forward and take on national expansion—would take a great deal of time, effort, and outside finances.

I knew that Portillo's had legs because of its popularity in other states. I wanted to see the brand all over the United States and I asked myself, "What's the best way to do that?" And there was another piece to the puzzle that I thought more of each day. I wanted to enjoy the fruits of this incredible success and, at 74 years old at the time, turn to other endeavors and adventures with my wife, children, and grand-children. There was no balance in my life, a trend that had started decades ago. I started attending more funerals than weddings and began to think about my own mortality. I wanted to spend more time on my boat and travel. That wasn't going to happen if I continued to own and oversee Portillo's.

But when I think back on that 2012–13 window, I am not joking when I said it seemed everywhere I turned in a Portillo's, there was Damon. I told him numerous times I didn't want to sell. I was having too much fun. Damon said, "You don't know the numbers we can get for you?" I countered, "You tell me the numbers you can get." Damon threw out a number and I answered, "It's not enough." He'd say, "How much do you want?" I told him not to worry about it because I didn't want to sell, that I needed to get back to the counter and wait on my customers.

That's where I felt at home, in a Portillo's on the front lines. I still loved the business, I loved the customers, I loved my employees. But the more Damon came around and the more we talked, I admitted to myself the timing seemed better and better. The national trend was like Pac-Man, that arcade game released in the 1980s where the yellow-colored character consumed all those dots. Companies were purchasing companies that had a positive cash flow and were sound financially.

Even more important to me was I had to make sure, if I decided to sell Portillo's, that it was to a buyer who didn't change the culture or change our methods with their own restaurant operating systems. I had worked too long and too hard to see that happen.

The decision to sell was a big, emotional moment for me, even to this day.

Berkshire Partners is an American private equity firm located in Boston. The company's website shares that it is a leading private investment firm with a track record of success spanning more than 30 years. Berkshire has raised nine private equity funds with more than $16 billion in aggregate capital commitments and manages a marketable securities fund, Stockbridge Investors, with more than $2.5 billion of capital.

I sold my 38 stores, which also included nine Barnelli's Pasta Bowl restaurants, all of which sit inside Portillo's properties, plus two commisaries, to Berkshire on August 1, 2014, for two reasons.

Number 1, I felt that they truly understood how special our brand and culture was.

Number 2, the company didn't have any restaurants in its portfolio. That was important to me because my hope was Berkshire embraced and learned Portillo's training methods and culture. If it were invested in other restaurants, the practices of those chains may bleed into ours.

Berkshire realized and understood Portillo's was a brand with legs. We had opened stores in Arizona and California. We shipped food to all 50 states.

I had two dozen suitors that wanted to purchase Portillo's. Berkshire didn't have the highest bid. I dismissed a higher offer because it included plans to quickly take Portillo's public. I thought that was a bad, bad idea. I thought the firm would make immediate changes, ruin the culture, and try to expand too quickly. In a span of 13 months I meticulously opened four restaurants, including two in Arizona, and a commissary without borrowing a dime.

Even a good friend of mine, Jimmy John Liautaud, wanted to purchase Portillo's. Jimmy founded Jimmy John's sandwich restaurant chain in 1983. It's headquartered in Champaign, Illinois, and in 30 years the company grew to more than 2,500 locations. But I told Jimmy, "I don't want you to bid on it. I don't care how much you give me." I wouldn't even give Jimmy our financial books to review. I told Jimmy his brand was much different than the Portillo's brand. I didn't want somebody to come in and change our formula. Jim and I are good friends today and I admire what he has done.

It is complex by design and it works. Remember when I explained about the moat I built around Portillo's? My moat is the complexity of the business and it helps keep the competition away.

I also have a funny story regarding the sale. I was out to dinner with two guys from Berkshire at RPM Italian, a downtown Chicago restaurant. It's owned by a friend, Rich Melman. Rich grew up in Chicago, and as a child, he sold ice cream and peanuts at the beaches and even sold eggs door to door, according to published accounts.

He's the founder of Lettuce Entertain You Enterprises, a privately held restaurant company with more than 100 venues.

Rich found out about my meeting with Berkshire so he and his two kids joined us at our table. Rich has got great instincts and common sense. So, Rich looked at the two guys from Berkshire and said, "You guys are smart. You probably got MBAs. You probably went to a really nice school and all that. See that guy next to me? Him and I are smart, too. We're a different kind of smart. You guys don't know anything about this business. You should listen to this guy," he said as he pointed toward me.

We all had a good laugh, but this was serious business to me. My approach was straightforward: when you open a restaurant and show up for work every day, you do whatever it takes to make sure that customer gets the best dog-gone service. That's the main difference between an MBA and a PhD. And you know what a PhD stands for? "Portillo's hot dogs." Rich is the best in his type of business and I admire and respect him very much.

When I met with all the private equity groups, I was prepared with the information on each person. Patty Sullivan would research the key players. Prior to the start of the meeting, I had their photograph, a history of their education, their title. I had everything. I thought that Chicago restaurant meeting with Berkshire—and after talking to the Berkshire representatives many, many times during the sales process—showed me they understood the culture.

I knew Portillo's was good. But I didn't really truly realize how great we were until all this attention started. When word got out that Portillo's was for sale, my god, 24 private equity groups knocked on my door. They were flying to Chicago on private jets and many times I had two meetings a day. And there were other people I wouldn't let in, like Jimmy John. And when Berkshire saw the returns and the money we were making, I don't think the company even believed it. It sent out its accountants from Boston to audit our books and they probably looked at me and thought, "Here is a guy with no real experts or accounting gurus and all that." And we had a better bottom line than anything they had ever seen. My bottom line was unbelievable because I was on top of everything. Any financial decision that was under $500, I allowed a Portillo's supervisor to clear. Anything over $500, I cleared it. I knew where every penny went.

The workload never overwhelmed me. I was a working fool. That's all I did but I loved it. My whole life was work. Was it overwhelming? No. I love busy. I juggled four, five, six things at once. I am still that way. I believed I was always good about getting my point across on how to run a business. And I think that always was what Berkshire wanted. How does Dick Portillo think? Because what I accomplished shouldn't have worked.

The Portillo Restaurant Group was the largest privately owned restaurant company in the Midwest prior to the sale. Combined, the concepts had more than 4,000 employees and nearly 50 businesses in four states, plus a catering and shipping division and shopping centers. This was all accomplished without franchising or investors. I attribute much of my success to my hard-working employees and to our satisfied customers.

I had a difficult and impoverished upbringing. But I loved to compete and, like that old saying, "Once a competitor, always a competitor." And that spilled into Portillo's from the first time I opened the window to greet customers from my 6' x 12' trailer. I never rested. I was always worried about who was behind me, and I fought to stay on top. I didn't have much when I started and I didn't want to lose what I had built. And I tried to instill that quality of ownership, culture, and teamwork into my team.

I have told Berkshire as long as it keeps the culture the way it is, it won't have any problems. Don't let the real estate department get ahead of the training department. It's a slow-moving process. It's a unique formula and store managers need experience, not only knowing how to make a sandwich, do inventory, and order product but also how to roll up their sleeves, bring everyone together, get them united behind the strategy to solve the problems, make sure they're invested, and work alongside them to make sure the work gets done. It all goes back to my time in the Marines.

Portillo's is a high-volume business. There's a lot of action. Employees are ringing up orders every 10 seconds, customers are asking questions, the noise and the atmosphere, maybe an employee didn't show for work or an important piece of equipment just broke. That's a lot of stress. I believe Berkshire is committed to living up to the standards we created. Whatever it does as a team, it has to keep driving and keep pushing things to the limit. There are so many companies out there that are trying to take a bite out of Portillo's. You have competitors who are trying to do hot dogs, trying to do chicken fingers, trying to do broiled chicken, trying to do salads, trying to do fish, and trying the little niche things we all do within our restaurant.

Many people in the fast-casual business wanted to know, "What gave you the balls to build something so big?" It did take balls. Nobody else has ever done what I have done. Nobody went from a sparse trailer to these 10,000- to 16,000- square feet restaurants with the unique décor and atmosphere. I needed that large size to give the customers the experience I thought they wanted. An experience that nobody else in the business can duplicate.

As you might imagine, once I sold the business my involvement in the day-to-day decision-making became limited. But even after selling the business, I continue to be a great customer. I try to stop in every restaurant I drive by because I am so proud of what we built. I still feel an incredible sense of pride when I visit a Portillo's. When I see people lined up in the store and cars in the drive-thru, I enjoy it. They are there because of what I did. It makes me feel good and I like being part of it.

On Portillo's 54th birthday bash in April 2017, the business celebrated by selling a slice of our famous chocolate cake for 54 cents. We sold about 150,000 slices of chocolate cake at 47 restaurants at the time in six states. And there were some customers who didn't get a slice because demand outpaced supply.

On the business side, I also own a substantial amount of Portillo's hot dogs real estate. As the landlord, Berkshire pays me rent.

The success I enjoy in Portillo's wasn't about me. It wasn't a single dimension. Restaurants are one of the last industries where you can take a kid who has no aptitude for anything yet, coming out of high school, and turn him into a professional success. And because of the way we train at Portillo's, we can teach that person to run a $10 million business, hire 200 people, and manage inventory, food, and staffing. Nobody else does that. You are learning a skill and a trade. Not everybody has to go to college. Restaurants are a great place to learn about yourself and life. It's not for everyone, but there's a lot of people who have gone into the restaurant business like a Portillo's and a lot of our employees are making six figures and enjoying a good life. I am very proud of that, too.

I still laugh when I think about the many times I saw Damon Chandik in the crowd at Portillo's. "Just happened to be stopping by again?" I asked. "Yeah, just driving by. When can we talk?" he said. I said, "Damon, we've been through this." But finally, we talked. And we finally settled on a price.

It was the right decision at the right time.

18
Moving Forward

As I've said from the beginning of this book, long lines don't impress me. Retirement doesn't either. For some, retirement might be a goal. I can't imagine truly being "retired."

In this phase of my life, I want to spend more time with my family and my grandchildren. I want to spend more time on my yacht and fishing—and why wouldn't I? I've got the best yacht captain in the industry, Wayne Nolander, and the best crew. I've got enough money, but, quite frankly, making money is still fun. And I have a lot of fun projects going on. It's not necessarily about money now. It's about the fun of doing something with my life that I enjoy.

I continue to love the challenges and excitement of business. Let everyone else play golf. So many of my friends spend hours and hours and hours chasing that little ball around the green. For what? I don't know. I don't see it. It looks boring. It's obviously not boring to people who play golf, but to me it looks boring. What happens once you get the ball in the hole? You chase the ball around to the next hole? I know golfers will cringe when I say this, but I don't find it interesting. I am crazy, I know!

Maybe that helps explain my mindset to this day. Even after the sale of Portillo's in 2014, I am still afraid of losing everything. That's still my greatest fear. To lose everything I have worked so hard for since I opened that hot dog stand in 1963.

That's why I am so diversified and I stay so busy.

As an entrepreneur, I got an early start in real estate by developing shopping centers for some of my Portillo's stores. I learned there was no security in leasing property from others. I wanted to be my own landlord. Maybe it's that fear again. I was looking for that security. An owner could say, "Portillo, we don't want to renew your lease. You're out of here." So that fear of somebody doing that led me to build my own security. If I owned the land, no one could kick me out.

I read somewhere that millennials are not buying homes. That got me interested in apartments, and now I own apartment properties in Texas, Florida, Georgia, and Kentucky, with almost 2,000 units combined. I own shopping centers in Oswego, Elgin, and Bolingbrook, all in Illinois, as well as one in Indianapolis. I also own nearly 4 million square feet of warehouse space in Indianapolis. I am involved in every step, from visiting properties to studying the local markets to reviewing the financials. I want to understand every facet of the deal.

I also have backed my daughter-in-law Gina—it's her chocolate cake recipe that is used at Portillo's—in purchasing, rehabbing, and selling large homes. I backed BlueRoad Ventures' $139 million acquisition of 48 single-tenant rental buildings in 18 states, including the Chicago area. I am an investor in other restaurants, including Gibsons Bar & Steakhouse in Oak Brook, and I am the majority owner in the Boathouse at Disney Springs in Orlando, which to this day is the highest-grossing restaurant in Disney Springs and, according to *USA Today*, the sixth-highest grossing restaurant in the United States. All the businesses I am blessed to be involved with can be found at the end of this book.

I still look at every day as a new challenge and I can't wait to get it started. You know how many investment opportunities come through my office every day? I turn down 95 percent of the proposals. I have to. But when all of a sudden one comes in that really interests me, I jump on it. People always tell me they have a great investment for me. It has to be unique. It has to be exciting. It has to be fun.

I am not doing this just for the money. I am having the time of my life as I near age 80.

My wealth has enabled me to be involved in important organizations, including the Chicago Diabetes Project, the Wounded Warrior Battalion at Marine Corps Base Camp Pendleton in California, and a Chicago-area home for abused women and children.

The Chicago Diabetes Project is extremely personal for me. That's because Sharon has Type I diabetes. Diabetes is when the body's immune system attacks part of its own pancreas. Nobody really knows why, but the immune system mistakenly sees the insulin-producing cells in the pancreas as foreign and destroys them. Diabetes develops when the pancreas does not make enough insulin, the body's cells do not use insulin effectively, or both. As a result, glucose builds up in the blood instead of being absorbed by cells in the body.

I have donated millions to the Chicago Diabetes Project, which, as explained on its website, is a global collaboration of scientists, researchers, physicians, and surgeons with one mission: to cure diabetes. The website explains that in recent years interest in diabetes has intensified on account of nearing epidemic proportions: in 1985 there were 30 million diabetics; today that number has rocketed to more than 170 million. By 2025, diabetes is likely to affect 300 million people worldwide.

Dr. Jose Oberholzer is the director of the Chicago Diabetes Project and a guy I really respect. One of these days they are going to build a monument to this guy and I hope they do, because he's going to find a cure for diabetes. He's close to finding a cure. More than eight years ago Sharon underwent an Islet Cell transplant. That is when isolated islets from a donor pancreas are injected into another person. Sharon is in need of another procedure. Sharon's blood type is very rare, just like everything else about her—special and rare.

When Portillo's expanded into California in 2005, a Marine officer asked me to provide a discount for meals served to those from the Wounded Warrior Battalion at Camp Pendleton. I told the officer I would provide the group with free meals, but I also asked for a favor. I wanted to see my old barracks from when I was a Marine. When I was escorted in, all the Marines stood and snapped to attention. It caught me off guard and I was surprised. I smiled and told them, "At ease."

I've also been able to financially help my high school alma mater, Argo Community High in Summit, Illinois. In August 2017, a ribbon-cutting ceremony was held for the $17.6 million Richard and Sharon Portillo Performing Arts Center. The 45,000-square-foot building has an auditorium with 430 seats, a band room, a prop shop, a chorale room, and rehearsal and dressing rooms. We pledged $1 million to the project in 2016, and that amount was expected to defray about $8 million in interest paid on loans for the project. Both Sharon and I were very pleased to make this donation to Argo.

Who would have ever thought a guy like me—Richard Portillo, Class of 1957—a guy who struggled in the classroom due to a learning disability, met my lovely wife in those hallways, played football and joined the Marines only days after graduation, would be listed among the school's notable alumni 60 years later? Check out Wikipedia. I am listed alongside the likes of Ted Kluszewski, who played most of his career with the Cincinnati Reds; Mamie Till, the fourth black graduate of Argo and mother of Emmett Till, whose murder served as a catalyst in the civil rights movement; Johnny Karras, a halfback for the Illinois team that won the 1952 Rose Bowl; and Saul White, a professional basketball player who currently travels the world entertaining fans as a member of the Harlem Globetrotters.

Argo holds a lot of fond memories for Sharon and me, and the connections last to this day. A teammate of mine on the football team, Jimmy Zwijack, has piloted my yacht. (He has since passed away.) Mike Van Ort was a classmate of mine who went on to fly with the Blue Angels. I named my eldest son Michael after him. It feels so good to be involved in projects such as the Performing Arts Center. According to Chicago media reports, our pledge to Argo makes me a member of a small group of wealthy Chicago entrepreneurs who donate to their high schools. Both Richard Driehaus—founder, chief investment officer, and chairman of Driehaus Capital Management—and Mellody Hobson, president of Ariel Investments, donate to St. Ignatius College Prep, where both attended high school. As for university donations, Citadel founder Ken Griffin donated $150 million to Harvard University, his alma mater, in 2014.

I love to travel and I love to read, and it's all tied into my keen interest in history.

Maybe it's childish, but I have often asked myself what it would have been like to live during a different era. What would I have done? How would I have acted? What did people then have to go through? How did they live? I have always tried to imagine myself in that era. I have never been able to trace my roots, though. My mother was born in Greece. My dad was born in Mexico but moved to El Paso, Texas, when he was young. And from El Paso he went to Dawson, New Mexico, where my grandmother worked for a mining camp. And that's as far back as I go. But I would like to know what happened before that. Where did they come from? I will never know.

I recently read a book about Theodore Roosevelt, who was a statesman, author, explorer, solider, and the 26th president of the United States. I couldn't put down the book. It was 360-something pages. I mean, every free moment that I had I was reading that book. But I felt that I was there with Roosevelt during his adventures. I almost felt what Theodore was feeling, because I have been in that type of a climate and in those jungles that were mentioned in the book. I was in Peleliu, I was in New Guinea, I was in Bougainville, the Solomon Islands. So, my mind went into that era as I read that book. One of the recent books I read and thoroughly enjoyed was on Thomas Jefferson and the Pirates of Tripoli. I also love Picasso. I read up a little bit about him and how he thought. He loved life, he loved women—although you'll never know it by some of the drawings that he has done. You'd think he hated women. He said he wanted to live like an adolescent until he was in his nineties, and he did. I would've loved to have met the guy.

I met some interesting people over the years, too. One of them was actor Anthony Quinn, who passed away in 2001. I loved the guy. My wife thought he was a male chauvinist, and maybe he was a little bit. But when he walked in a room and talked to you, it was special. And for some reason, he liked me and we got along good, otherwise I wouldn't have been invited to his 85th birthday party. He'd walk in a room and there was something about him. I have a portrait of Quinn in our home that he painted.

During one of my early journeys to Cuba, I met Gregorio Fuentes, a fisherman and captain of the *Pilar*, the boat that belonged to American writer Ernest Hemingway. (Hemingway was born in Oak Park, Illinois, by the way.) Hemingway's book, *The Old Man and the Sea*, was written about Fuentes. Gregorio migrated to Cuba when he was 22 and he and Hemingway were very, very close. When you get two guys on a boat that go out there for weeks at a time, they get close, you know what I mean? So, Gregorio knew Hemingway and he knew him really well. I met Gregorio, who died in 2002 at the age of 104, and we had an interesting conversation about Hemingway, who died in 1961. For Hemingway's *For Whom the Bell Tolls*, Hemingway took his experiences in the Spanish Civil War and wrote a book on it. I didn't realize that until later on in life: I did pretty much the same thing, only I didn't write a book until now. I built a restaurant.

I can't get enough of traveling either. I love the western United States. The Keys are a favorite stop. But one of the most unique trips I have taken was in 2015, when I went to the island of Bougainville in Papua New Guinea. That's where Japanese Marshall Admiral Isoroku Yamamoto died in a plane crash after a fight with American aircraft on April 18, 1943. Yamamoto was responsible for planning the attack on Pearl Harbor during World War II. I funded an expedition to the island and as we viewed the plane wreckage from that crash, a retired professor on the trip with me, Anderson Giles, caught sight of a gold tooth in the mud nearby. Giles recalled that Yamamoto was shot in the jaw during the air attack. The locals on the island own the wreckage site, and the clan chief confiscated the tooth. I later negotiated with the chief and purchased the tooth for $14,000. While many believe the chances that it actually is Yamamoto's tooth are slim to none, I am hopeful DNA left in the tooth could be extracted for verification. My goal with the tooth is to make a documentary regarding my trip in finding it and then eventually turn it over to the Japanese government. That would be fun.

It has been so exciting to build something and do something different in life. I think it is the entrepreneur's curse that it's not even about money. It's not even about the number of employees, it's not even about the number of restaurants. The next challenge excites me in ways that security and safety does not.

After we sold Portillo's to Berkshire Partners, reality set it. I was worth over a billion dollars that day. But was my life going to change? Not really. The morning following our sale, I woke up the same time as I always did, at 5:00 AM. I looked at Sharon and said, "Look what we did with $1,100 and lots of passion, hard work, and sacrifice."

Then we hugged.

God Bless America.

Appendix
Real Estate and
Other Investments

Restaurant Real Estate

Honey Jam Café in Downers Grove & Bolingbrook, IL

Miller's Ale House in Aurora, IL

Andy's Frozen Custard in Bolingbrook, IL

Denny's in Batavia, IL

Portillo's Hot Dogs; 21 Restaurants and two commissary locations

Restaurant Investments

The Boathouse Restaurant in Disney Springs, FL; Ranked sixth-
highest-grossing restaurant in the U.S.

Gibson's Steakhouse in Oak Brook, IL

RPM Italian in Washington, D.C.

Summer House in North Bethesda, MD

Stella Barra Pizzeria in North Bethesda, MD

Shopping Centers
Julian's Plaza in Bolingbrook, IL
Prairie Market in Oswego, IL
Richport Commons in Elgin, IL
Richport Plaza in Elgin, IL
Tri-Land Southern Plaza in Indianapolis, IN

Multi-Family Housing
1,939 apartment units across the United States

Residential Real Estate
Portillo's Home Development; Residential Real Estate in Illinois &
    Florida
Highland Hustle; Residential Real Estate in Illinois

Other Investments
$5 million invested in Uber
Hayden Flour Mill; a historic hotel/retail/office development in
    Tempe, AZ
Wash-U Car Wash; seven Locations in Illinois
Industrial Warehouse Portfolio; seven buildings and 3.9 million square
    feet in Indianapolis, IN
Fulton Market District; five properties in Chicago, IL
BlueRoad Net Lease Portfolio; Including 48 retail and restaurant
    buildings in 18 states
BlueRoad Ventures; An alternative asset management and investment
    company

Private Equity Funds
TCP Lending Fund
Berkshire Fund IX
Huizenga Managers Fund